Social Issues
in Literature

Social and Psychological Disorder in the Works of Edgar Allan Poe

Other Books in the Social Issues in Literature Series:

Social Issues
in Literature

Social and Psychological Disorder in the Works of Edgar Allan Poe

Claudia Durst Johnson, Book Editor

GREENHAVEN PRESS
A part of Gale, Cengage Learning

GALE
CENGAGE Learning

Detroit • New York • San Francisco • New Haven, Conn • Waterville, Maine • London

Christine Nasso, *Publisher*
Elizabeth Des Chenes, *Managing Editor*

For more information, contact:
Greenhaven Press
27500 Drake Rd.
Farmington Hills, MI 48331-3535
Or you can visit our Internet site at gale.cengage.com

Articles in Greenhaven Press anthologies are often edited for length to meet page require-ments. In addition, original titles of these works are changed to clearly present the main thesis and to explicitly indicate the author's opinion. Every effort is made to ensure that Greenhaven Press accurately reflects the original intent of the authors. Every effort has been made to trace the owners of copyrighted material.

Cover image © Pictorial Press Ltd./Alamy.

LIBRARY OF CONGRESS CATALOGING-IN-PUBLICATION DATA

Social and psychological disorder in the works of Edgar Allan Poe / Claudia Durst Johnson, book editor.
    p. cm. -- (Social issues in literature)
    Includes bibliographical references and index.
    ISBN 978-0-7377-5016-4 (hardcover) -- ISBN 978-0-7377-5017-1 (pbk.)
    1. Poe, Edgar Allan, 1809-1849--Criticism and interpretation--Juvenile literature.
2. Social problems in literature--Juvenile literature. I. Johnson, Claudia Durst, 1938- II. Series: Social issues in literature.
   PS2638.S63 2010
   818'.309--dc22
                                     2010000083

Printed in the United States of America
2 3 4 5 6   15 14 13 12 11

FD304

As sense after sense is taken away, the character in "The Pit and the Pendulum" loses his will and sanity. Only then does the hand reach out to save him.

Chapter 3: Contemporary Instances of Death and Abnormal Psychology

The insanity defense has been employed in trials such as that of Sheila LaBarre, who believed she was an angel sent by God to kill her two lovers. Juries, however, rarely find killers not guilty by reason of insanity.

Introduction

October 2009 marked the two hundredth year since the birth of Edgar Allan Poe, whose writing ended with his death in 1849, at the young age of thirty-nine. The lasting significance of Poe as a pivotal figure in his portraits of social and psychological disorders, not to mention his stature as a gothic cult figure, is seen in the extent of the public celebration of his life so many years later. In July 2009 a paper about impulses that often lead, through various stages, to violence, was published in *Science* by psychologist Daniel M. Wegner. Wegner quoted extensively from Poe's "Imp of the Perverse." The year was also marked by two collections of tales in honor of Poe and a new biography of Poe by Peter Ackroyd. Poe was also celebrated in a six-page article on April 27, 2009, in one of the country's most prestigious magazines, *The New Yorker*. Finally, the *New York Times* reported that Poe was being honored 150 years after his death with two funeral services in Baltimore on October 7 and 8. Although he was a well-known figure when he died, only ten people attended his funeral in 1849. By contrast, hundreds of people attended the ceremonies in his honor in 2009. On October 8, an all-night vigil was held in Baltimore's Westminster Graveyard.

Poe's importance has sprung principally from his rendering of disturbed characters operating outside the realm of normal society. Whether mental disorders were the result of the supernatural (spirits and ghouls) or the brain (that could be examined scientifically) was a continuing controversy in Poe's time and throughout the twentieth century. Many critics and psychologists believe that Poe was actually a forerunner of the modern psychology that most notably surfaced with Sigmund Freud and Carl Jung in the early twentieth century. This is not altogether implausible, for Poe's classical education in England would have familiarized him with early Greek and

Roman notions of the unconscious. He undoubtedly was familiar with the French philosopher René Descartes (1516–1650), who had probed into the human personality and raised questions about the relationship between body and mind. Another thinker, English physician Thomas Willis (1621–1675) was well known for studying the pathology of the brain and wrote the first volume on medical psychology, addressing the maladies of melancholia, hypochondria, and hysteria as they are related to the mind.

Another influential figure in the seventeenth century, philosopher John Locke (1632–1704), an antiauthoritarian, challenged the theories that mental disorders were caused by the supernatural. The French School of psychology from the seventeenth to the nineteenth centuries continued to bring supernaturalism and spiritualism into the discussion of human personality. These scholars flatly repudiated the idea that psychology was a science. In short, they contended that personality disorders had more to do with ghosts and spirits than with the brain and human experience.

In Poe's own day, the best-known psychologist was Anton Mesmer, (1735–1815), who popularized hypnosis and phrenology, the latter being the practice of analyzing and healing personality disorders by examining the bumps on the patient's head.

By 1892 Sigmund Freud (1856–1939) had used the word "psychoanalysis" for the first time, treated sex as an issue in mental disorders, and more fully developed the idea of the unconscious. Today modern psychology is seen to be at the core of many nineteenth-century works of literature. Robert Louis Stevenson's *Dr. Jekyll and Mr. Hyde* (1886) and Bram Stoker's *Dracula* (1897) are two of the leading examples.

Indeed, gothic literature, which inevitably calls to mind the works of Edgar Allan Poe, had been relished by the reading and play-going public for centuries. However, only in the second half of the twentieth century were its psychological el-

ements recognized, including those in Poe's tales and poems. Gothic topics include murder, ghosts, witches, werewolves, vampires, monsters, imprisonment, ruins, sick nostalgia for the past, unnatural parents, haunted or decayed quarters, isolation, imprisonment, specters, forebodings, deformity, magic, dark and forbidding secrets, sexual violence, rape, incest, and, most important, cultural and mental decay.

Authors of the articles in this book investigate the gothic disorders outside the social norm as seen in Poe's life, in his work, and in our contemporary world. In each category critics see the mental sickness as coming not from supernatural elements outside of the real world but from inside society and the individual. In Chapter 1, biographers explain the irregularities of abuse in Poe's early life that would lead to his being labeled (and calling himself) mad shortly before he died.

In Chapter 2, critics analyze the psychological disorders in Poe's gothic works:

Obsession

Sick fixation on the past

Architectural and personal ruins

Motiveless Murder

Fear

Ghosts and spirits

Split personalities

Sadism

A relationship of mental derangement to love, death, reality, and art

The relationship that Poe's characters have to society is integral to their derangement. Most fail to engage society in any way, operating without social controls and standards, instead following an isolated ego that leads them to ghastly behavior. In other ways, characters emerge off-balance from a twisted society. Society shapes the minds of these mad narrators. This

is particularly true in their obsession with women. Poe's society regarded women as either angels or harlots: there was no middle territory. Poe's characters' attitudes toward women were also ambiguous. They either feared women's strength or idealized their perfection.

Another social matter that had a bearing on Poe was the controversy over the legal-insanity plea. He knew of contemporary court cases in which lawyers defended murderers on the grounds of insanity. The reader is led to speculate whether any of his criminals actually realize that their actions are wrong and are, therefore, innocent by reason of insanity.

The relentless madness in our twenty-first-century society, similar to that in Poe's poetry and fiction, is explored in Chapter 3.

Chronology

1809

Edgar Poe is born in Boston, the son of traveling actors David and Elizabeth Poe.

1811

Poe's mother and father die within weeks of each other, and John and Frances Allan take in Poe and raise him, although they never formally adopt him.

1815

After two years of schooling, the Allans move to England, where Poe attends school and receives a classical education.

1820

Poe and the Allans return to the United States, where his schooling continues.

1827

Poe fights with John Allan, who refuses to pay Poe's gambling debts. Poe subsequently leaves the University of Virginia and his home in Richmond. He moves to Baltimore, where he has other family. His first book, *Tamerlane and Other Poems*, is published. He enlists in the U.S. Army under the name of Edgar A. Perry and is stationed at Fort Moultrie on Sullivan's Island off the coast of Charleston, South Carolina.

1829

After his outfit is moved to Fort Monroe, Virginia, Poe is promoted to sergeant-major of his regiment. His foster mother, Frances Allan, dies. He manages a release from the army and publishes his second book, *Al Aaraaf, Tamerlane, and Minor Poems*.

1830

Poe enters West Point, the United States Military Academy, as a cadet.

1831

Disillusioned, he refuses to do his duties and is court-martialed and dismissed from West Point. His *Poems* is published.

1834

Poe's foster father, John Allan, dies, leaving Poe out of his will.

1835–1839

Poe edits several literary magazines and publishes his work in magazines.

1836

At the age of twenty-seven, Poe marries his cousin, Virginia, who is thirteen.

1838

After several moves, Poe, his wife, and his wife's mother settle in Philadelphia. *The Narrative of Arthur Gordon Pym of Nantucket* is published by Harper and Brothers.

1839–1846

Poe struggles to make a living by editing literary magazines and publishing stories and poems in journals. He also begins giving lectures.

1840

Two volumes of *Tales of the Grotesque and Arabesque* are published.

1844

Poe and his family move to New York City.

1845

"The Raven," his most acclaimed poem, is published in *The Evening Mirror*. *Tales* and *The Raven and Other Poems* are published by Wiley and Putnam.

1847

Poe's wife, Virginia, dies of tuberculosis.

1849

After two years of being plagued by poverty, unsuccessful love affairs, and alcoholism, Poe dies under mysterious circumstances in Baltimore.

Social Issues in Literature

Edgar Allan Poe's Background

The Life of Edgar Allan Poe

Eric W. Carlson

Eric W. Carlson, English professor emeritus at the University of Connecticut, Storrs, has written several books on Edgar Allan Poe and has been active in the Poe Society.

In the following essay Carlson makes the statement, contrary to most Poe biographers, that Poe was neither an alcoholic nor a drug addict, though he went through prolonged periods of relentless drunkenness. Poe and his family situation were both unstable. Still, he received an excellent academic education before college. Poe's failure at the University of Virginia derived from his attempt to sustain the lifestyle of the rest of the patrician students there. When his foster father refused him money to pay his gambling debts, he was forced to withdraw from the university. It was then that Poe turned to writing as a vocation. Carlson labels Poe's first period romantic and sees his second period as dominated by death and chaos. By the mid 1840s, two volumes of Poe's stories had appeared as collections. Just before his life ended, rather mysteriously, Poe had reason to hope for better things.

Ever since Poe's short stories first began to appear in the 1830s readers have been intrigued by the nature of the man or the mind that produced them. Was he as demonic or demented as the protagonists of his horror tales, and as analytical or psychic as the heroes of his detective and mystery stories? Contrary to popular legend, Poe was neither an alcoholic nor a drug addict, though he did struggle during much of his adult life against a predisposition to drink during periods of stress and despair. A highly complex character, Poe was

Eric W. Carlson, *American Short-Story Writers Before 1880*. Detroit, MI: Gale Research Inc., 1988. Copyright © 1988 by Gale Research Company. Reproduced by permission of Gale, a part of Cengage Learning.

capable of the strictest artistic control and intellectual acumen, at other times suffering from emotional instability and dependence.

A Sad but Privileged Childhood

Born in Boston on 19 January 1809, he was not yet three when his mother died on 8 December 1811 in Richmond. A talented leading lady in the American theater of the day, Elizabeth Arnold Poe, of English birth, had married David Poe, Jr., a mediocre actor who later abandoned his family. After his mother's death Poe was taken in by the childless John and Frances Allan; brother William Henry was taken in by his paternal grandparents; and sister Rosalie was cared for by foster parents. Allan, a Scottish-born tobacco merchant, was as strict and unemotional as his wife was overindulgent. When Allan's business interests took him to Scotland and London in 1815, Mrs. Allan and Poe accompanied him, returning to Richmond in 1820. Poe was educated in private academies, excelling in Latin, in writing verse, and declamation. He enjoyed swimming, skating, and shooting. In 1825 Allan inherited the sizable fortune of his uncle, William Gault; even so, being the child of former actors, Poe was regarded as an outsider by the Richmond elite. At sixteen, young Poe fell in love with Sarah Elmira Royster, to whom he became "engaged" without parental consent.

In February 1826 Poe entered the University of Virginia, where he excelled in Greek, Latin, French, Spanish, and Italian. When his allowance from Allan did not cover the cost of books and clothes, Poe resorted to playing cards for money, incurring debts of two thousand dollars. Refusing to pay these "debts of honor" at the end of the term in December, Allan withdrew Poe from the university. When all attempts at reconciliation with Allan failed, Poe went to Baltimore in March 1827, then sailed to Boston, where in May he enlisted in the United States Army as "Edgar A. Perry" and was assigned to

Contents

duty with the coast artillery at Fort Independence, Boston Harbor and later at Fort Moultrie on Sullivan's Island in Charleston Harbor. It was in Boston that a young printer was persuaded to publish Poe's anonymous first book, *Tamerlane and Other Poems. By a Bostonian* (1827). After Mrs. Allan died in February 1829, Poe quit the army and sought help in getting an appointment to West Point. A second volume, with six new poems, was published under Poe's own name in Baltimore in December 1829. On 1 July 1830 he entered West Point, but by October, learning that Allan had remarried and despairing of reconciliation or inheritance (he had never been legally adopted), Poe ignored orders, thus obtaining his dismissal from the academy on 31 January 1831.

Three Periods of Writing

Poe's writing career falls into three major periods, each marked by a shift in perspective. During the first period, 1827 to 1831, his three slim volumes of poetry expressed a strong attachment to the romantic myth of a pastoral and poetic ideal, made up of "dreams" and "memories" of a pristine paradise or Eden. These early poems celebrated Beauty and Innocence, Love and Joy as dynamic life values in the poet's feeling for the potential of harmony of mind with nature, of the "soul" with "God" or the universal "Ens" [i.e., Being]. In 1831, a transition year, three of Poe's poems ("Romance," "Israfel," and "To Helen") expressed a new commitment to a poetry of heartfelt conviction in the face of life's burdens and sorrows. During the decade that followed, 1831 to 1841, a radical change was reflected in poems and tales on the theme of death as a finality in a cosmic void of darkness and silence. His third and final period, 1841 to 1849, was marked by a return to poetry and by essays and fiction on the theme of psychic transcendentalism. Through all three of these stages Poe continued to publish comic and satiric tales, mainly parodies, burlesques, grotesques, and hoaxes. . . .

Author Edgar Allan Poe explores social and psychological disorders in many of his works. AP Images.

Literary Beginnings and Marriage

Although little is known of Poe's activities throughout 1832, in May 1833 he proposed for publication "Eleven Tales of the Arabesque," consisting of five *Saturday Courier* tales plus six new stories which were submitted to a contest sponsored by the *Baltimore Saturday Visiter*. The first prize of fifty dollars went to Poe's "MS. Found in a Bottle," which was published on 19 October, and an honorary second prize to his poem

"The Coliseum," The eleven tales "are supposed to be read at table," Poe explained to Joseph T. and *Edwin Buckingham*, editors of the *New-England Magazine*, "by the eleven members of a literary club, and are followed by the remarks of the company upon each. These remarks are intended as a burlesque upon criticism. In the whole, originality more than anything else has been attempted . . ." As representative of the collection, Poe enclosed "Epimanes" (*Messenger*, March 1836; republished as "Four Beasts in One—The Homo-Cameleopard," *Broadway Journal*, 6 December 1845), a story for which he drew upon both ancient and modern history, only the main incident being an invention. Although Jacksonianism [political philosophy of President Andrew Jackson] may have been an intended target, the satire is less applicable to American democracy than to monarchical regimes. An overlooked aspect of the story is the point of view, the use of a witness-reporter who, like a modern-day "eye-witness" newscaster, describes the unfolding event in the dramatic tones of one who is baffled, amazed, and finally (and ironically) caught up in the crowd's hysterical celebration. . . .

Meanwhile, Poe had married his cousin Virginia Clemm on 16 May 1836; she was not quite fourteen. Poe had been living in the Clemm house-hold, consisting of Virginia, her mother, Maria Clemm, and Poe's grandmother, Elizabeth Poe, since 1831. After the grandmother's death in 1835 Poe and the Clemms moved from Baltimore to Richmond. In February 1837, with Mrs. Clemm, Poe and Virginia moved to New York, where they stayed for about a year and a half before relocating in Philadelphia. . . .

The Tale of Psychic Excitement

In January 1842 Virginia Poe suffered her first attack of tuberculosis, placing her health in jeopardy for years, during which Poe agonized with every relapse. In May Poe resigned the editorship at *Graham's Magazine* that he had held since April

1841. In his third essay on Nathaniel Hawthorne, for the November 1847 issue of *Godey's Lady's Book*, Poe composed a discriminating and revealing definition of originality as something more than novelty: "true originality . . . is that which, in bringing out the half-formed, the reluctant, or the unexpressed fancies of mankind, or in exciting the more delicate pulses of the heart's passion, or in giving birth to some universal sentiment or instinct in embryo, thus combines with the pleasurable effect of *apparent* novelty, a real egoistic delight," leaving the reader to feel that he and the author "have, together, created this thing." Even allegory—which is usually to be avoided—if "properly handled, judiciously subdued, seen only as a shadow or by suggestive glimpses" may fulfill the function of the tale, namely to stimulate the reader to intense, psychic excitement. Most famous of all is this definition:

> A skilful artist has constructed a tale. He has not fashioned the thoughts to accommodate his incidents, but having deliberately conceived a certain *single effect* to be wrought, he then invents such incidents, he then combines such events, and discusses them in such tone as may best serve him in establishing this preconceived effect. If his very first sentence tend not to the out-bringing of this effect, then in his very first step has he committed a blunder. In the whole composition there should be no word written of which the tendency, direct or indirect, is not to the one preestablished design. And by such means, with such care and skill, a picture is at length painted which leaves in the mind of him who contemplates it with a kindred art, a sense of the fullest satisfaction.

Taken alone, this definition may seem to relate only to rational art, in which everything is preconceived, but if taken with the definition of "true originality" above, it describes the organic nature of subconsciously determined creative art—as in the symbolic and impressionistic "tales of effect." . . .

Successes, Failures, and Depression

Still suffering from economic hardship, in March 1843 Poe went to Washington in search of a government job, but the search came to naught because of a drinking spree. Friends put the penniless Poe on the train for Philadelphia. In June, however, he became instantly famous when his story "The Gold Bug" won a one-hundred-dollar prize offered by the *Dollar Newspaper*. It appeared on 21 and 28 July in two installments and was often reprinted and even dramatized. In July *The Prose Romances of Edgar A. Poe*, the first of a pamphlet series, reprinted "The Murders in the Rue Morgue" (which first appeared in the April 1841 issue of *Graham's Magazine*) and "The Man That Was Used Up." During the winter months Poe lectured in several cities on poetry in America. . . .

The Poes returned to New York City in April 1844, and during the next five years Poe wrote such famous poems as "The Raven," "Ulalume," "For Annie," and "Annabel Lee." The popularity of "The Raven," which was often reprinted, parodied, and anthologized, made Poe more famous. *Graham's Magazine* for February 1845 carried James Russell Lowell's long essay-appreciation of Poe, praising him as "the most discriminating, philosophical and fearless critic upon imaginative works who has written in America." Aided by Lowell, Poe became editor of the *Broadway Journal*, for which he wrote over sixty reviews and essays, a few new stories, and in which he reprinted revised versions of his tales and poems. By fall he had, with borrowed money, bought the journal, but when it lost money, Poe, ill and depressed, stopped publication early in January 1846. In 1845, also, two volumes of his work were published: *Tales by Edgar A. Poe*, containing twelve stories selected by Evert A. Duyckinck, and, in November, *The Raven and Other Poems*. . . .

After Virginia's Death

In 1846, with Poe only irregularly employed, the family suffered from economic hardship, illness, and depression. . . . Virginia died of consumption on 30 January 1847. During her final illness, Poe, with "the horrible never-ending oscillation between hope and despair," tried to drown his grief in alcohol. Despite his continuing illness, Poe produced tales, essays, reviews, and poems.

In 1848 Poe lectured on "The Poetic Principle" and *Eureka*. Now more in need of emotional security than ever, he developed romantic friendships with several women, notably Sarah Helen Whitman, Mrs. Annie Richmond, and Mrs. Elmira Shelton (formerly Sarah Elmira Royster, his former fiancee); these platonic friendships are echoed in some of the poems and letters, but not in the fiction. Poe's conditional engagement to the forty-five-year-old Mrs. Whitman was ended when he . . . called on her after drinking. Years later she published *Edgar Poe and His Critics* (1860), a sympathetic defense of Poe as person and writer. Poe's final year, 1849, was divided among lecturing, writing poetry and narrative, and visiting friends, old and new, in Philadelphia, Richmond, and Baltimore. Two months in Richmond were his happiest; there he visited Mrs. Shelton, now a widow, who apparently accepted his marriage proposal. Seemingly in fair health when leaving Richmond for New York to fetch Maria Clemm, he stopped in Baltimore and several days later, on election day, 3 October, was found "extremely ill," half conscious and delirious, outside a polling place. On 7 October he died.

The Sources of Poe's Youthful Despair

Jeffrey Meyers

A native New Yorker, Jeffrey Meyers is a former professor and now a prolific and distinguished biographer living in Berkeley, California. He is one of only a dozen Americans who are fellows of the British Royal Society of Literature.

Edgar Allan Poe's childhood was not likely to leave him with a healthy state of mind, writes Meyers in the following essay. Poe's poverty-stricken actress mother died when he was two years old, and his foster father despised and refused to support him. Poe had a shaky start into young manhood, failing at everything he attempted, including completing educations at the University of Virginia and West Point. Even though he was extremely learned and had genteel manners, he was crippled by his own egotism, tending toward self-destruction and drunkenness. A turn in his life came when he connected with his father's widowed sister and her daughter, Virginia, whom he eventually married. They suffered through poverty together until Virginia's early death. The young Poe unsuccessfully tried to pull himself out of poverty by selling stories and criticism and establishing literary magazines, but he made enemies instead of money.

Born in poverty, the child of a broken home, and orphaned at the age of two; unable to complete his university education, expelled from West Point and rejected by his foster father; traumatized by the deaths of the women who had loved him—Eliza Poe, Jane Stanard and Frances Allan—Poe was well prepared for a perfectly wretched life. Despite all efforts to improve his fortunes, his descent into the lower class was to

prove permanent. This celebrated delinquent became the sad-
dest and strangest figure in American literature. . . . He kept
no diaries, had no intimate friends and confided in no one.

A Caustic Character

Poe's strange, melancholy loneliness, his obsession with plagiarism, his sensitivity to criticism, his frequent requests for
money, his threats of rash behavior, his overweening pride, his
humiliating self-abasement and his compulsive self-destruction
all contributed to his caustic and corrosive character. Yet his
sense of social grievance, his brooding temperament, his feck-
lessness, his excitable, imperious nature were balanced by his
Castilian courtesy, "polished manners, enormous erudition,
formidable conversational abilities, and indescribable personal
magnetism."

The life of the "wild, eccentric, audacious, tortured, horror-
haunted, sorrowing, beauty-loving" Poe [as Daniel Hoffman
describes him] was defined by the unbearable tensions in his
paradoxical character. He was a Virginia gentleman and the
son of itinerant actors, the heir to a great fortune and a disin-
herited outcast, a university man who had failed to graduate,
a soldier bought out of the army, a court-martialed cadet.
Later in life he would become a husband with an unapproach-
able child-bride, a brilliant editor and low-salaried hack, a
world-renowned but impoverished author, the fiancé of two
women who would not marry him, a normally temperate man
and an uncontrollable alcoholic, a rationalist with a mystical
cast of mind, a materialist who yearned for a final unity with
God.

The sharp inward division between the impressive force of
Poe's rational mind and the overpowering strength of his irrational apprehension was reflected not only in his poems and
stories but also in his conflict with authority, his anxious welcome of personal disaster and his sad compulsion to destroy
his own life. . . .

Poe quarreled with nearly everyone he ever met and alienated nearly everyone who was capable of helping him. Though sadly dependent upon patronage, his touchy pride and deep hostility to paternal authority led to consistently uneasy relations with his superiors: with John Allan (who intensified Poe's instability by refusing to define his status and expectations [by not legally adopting him]), with the officials at the university and the officers at West Point, and with the magazine owners who exploited his talent and paid subsistence wages—with anyone, in fact, who impugned his dignity, status or genius. Prompted by memories of his early oppression, he once shocked a listener by exclaiming, with satanic pride: "My whole nature utterly *revolts* at the idea that there is any Being in the Universe superior to *myself!*" But, till the very end of his life, he was forced to apologize to figures of authority and to explain the reasons for his irresponsibility, his poverty and his drunkenness. . . .

Genius and Madness

Since his opinions and speculations would differ wildly from those of *all* mankind—that he would be considered a madman, is evident. His consciousness of intellectual superiority, especially when he was confined to a humble position, inspired the enmity or mockery of ordinary men. There was a limited tolerance in journalistic circles for Poe's odd character, intellectual arrogance and pretentious learning.

In "Eleonora" Poe discussed a related idea—which had begun with Plato and evolved through the centuries to the Romantic poets—that genius was connected to madness, that the diseased imagination could transcend intellect and create the deepest artistic visions: "the question is not yet settled, whether madness is or is not the loftiest intelligence—whether much that is glorious—whether all that is profound—does not spring from disease of thought—from *moods* of mind exalted at the expense of the general intellect."

The unusually intelligent and extremely neurotic Poe was driven by what he called "the human thirst for self-torment." Defining the reasons for his own irrational behavior in "The Imp of the Perverse," he wrote that some men were motivated by self-destructive impulses, that "the assurance of the wrong or error of any action is often the one unconquerable *force* which impels us, and alone impels us to its prosecution." His own unhappy life—as well as that of his fictional characters— seemed dominated by this fatal principle. The guilt-obsessed narrator of "The Black Cat," for example, is also possessed by this profound and apparently inexplicable impulse: "The spirit of perverseness, I say, came to my final overthrow . . . this un- fathomable longing of the soul *to vex itself*—to offer violence to its own nature—to do wrong for wrong's sake only."

The unbearable tensions in Poe's divided personality led him to perversely self-destructive behavior, to conflict with authority and sometimes to morbid despair. He would com- municate this dark mood to his correspondents in an attempt to elicit their pity and sympathy; and kindly friends would of- fer encouragement and try to coax him out of his melancholy. One of them [John P. Kennedy] advised Poe to "subdue this brooding and boding inclination of your mind." Another [Anne C. Lynch Botta] insisted that "life is too short & there is too much to be done in it, to give one time to *despair*," and urged him to "exorcise that devil, I beg of you, as speedily as possible." . . .

A New Family

During his years in Baltimore, the least documented and most obscure period of his life, Poe lived in humble and sometimes desperate circumstances. He rediscovered his family and shared quarters with his father's widowed sister, Aunt Maria Clemm, and her child, his nine-year-old cousin Virginia, who would later become his wife. Born in 1790, Maria had in 1817 mar- ried William Clemm, a socially prominent Baltimore widower whose late wife was Maria's first cousin. Maria had three children, one of whom died in infancy. At the time of Clemm's death in 1826, his property had disappeared, and his widow (like Poe) was left desolate and unprotected. When Poe joined the household in May 1831—four months after his court-martial and the same month he published his third volume of poems in New York—Maria was barely managing to support herself by sewing, by keeping occasional boarders in her tiny house and by a $240 annual pension, paid to her paralyzed, bedridden mother, Elizabeth, the widow of "General" Poe.

The large, forty-one-year-old Maria Clemm had the face and figure of a man. A daguerreotype portrays her in a white widow's bonnet with long streamers, trim white collar and pleated black dress. She had a large forehead, deep-set, widely spaced eyes with overhanging brows, a broad nose, lined cheeks, long narrow mouth, firm chin and puffy jowls. The kindly, energetic and tactless Maria was absolutely devoted to Poe. She believed in his genius, cared for him with a maternal solicitude and willingly made great sacrifices on his behalf. . . .

A New Mother

Poe was closer to Maria than to anyone else he ever knew. His intense emotional attachment to both Maria and Virginia Clemm was forged when, rejected by his foster father, he had returned to his own blood relations, to the aunt and cousin who comprised his third family. Maria too had suffered bereavement, having lost her husband and child. Poe's deeply felt though somewhat morbid and sentimental sonnet, "To My Mother," is dedicated not to Eliza Poe or Frances Allan, who were never entirely satisfactory mothers, but to Maria Clemm.

Acclaim

In June 1833 the Baltimore *Saturday Visiter* . . . offered two prizes in order to encourage literature and procure the finest works for their readers: fifty dollars for the best tale in prose and twenty-five dollars for the best short poem. Poe submitted a poem, "The Coliseum," and six tales: "Four Beasts in One," "Lionizing," "Silence," "The Assignation," "A Descent into the Maelström" and "MS. Found in a Bottle." The last story won the prize. In announcing the winner, the judges defined the characteristic qualities of Poe's works and justly stated that "these tales are eminently distinguished by a wild, vigorous and poetical imagination, a rich style, a fertile invention, and varied and curious learning." . . .

Quarrels over Plagiarism

Though Poe was always quick to accuse others of plagiarism, his early stories reveal that he too cannibalized his literary ancestors. He adopted four major conventions from the influential Scottish monthly, *Blackwood's Magazine*: "the creation of a literary personality, the 'self-consciously learned pose,' the exploitation of the hoax, and the burlesque and horror tale as major fictional modes." In addition to borrowings from *Blackwood's*, [Ludwig] Tieck, [E.T.A.] Hoffmann, [Samuel Taylor] Coleridge and [Isaac] D'Israeli, Poe—early and late in his career—also appropriated material from [John] Milton, Thomas Moore, [Lord] Byron, [Percy Bysshe] Shelley, [John] Keats, Thomas Hood, Elizabeth Barrett and Alfred Tennyson. As he told his fellow poet James Russell Lowell: "I am profoundly excited by music, and by some poems—those by Tennyson especially—whom, with Keats, Shelley, Coleridge (occasionally) and a few others of like thought and expression, I regard as the *sole* poets." Yet Poe, at once derivative and original, both absorbed and transformed the work of his predecessors. He recognized sympathetic temperaments in past writers and discovered in them forms of expression that could be reaffirmed and recreated. . . .

Seeking Support

Poe's pressing need for money, sense of responsibility to Maria and Virginia Clemm, and all-too-human concern for his own uncertain future inspired a final attempt at reconciliation with John Allan. In April 1833, after a fifteen-month silence, the outcast wrote a last, futile letter. He did not mention his recent literary success, but hoped to arouse Allan's sense of pity and charity: "I am perishing—absolutely perishing for want of aid. And yet I am not idle—nor addicted to any vice—nor have I committed any offense against society which would render me deserving of so hard a fate. For God's sake pity me, and save me from destruction."

When this letter failed to elicit a response from his cold-hearted Pa, Poe tried a direct confrontation. On February 14, 1834, when Allan was seriously ill with dropsy, Poe returned to Richmond for a final visit. According to his childhood friend Thomas Ellis, Louisa Allan opened the door herself:

> A man of remarkable appearance stood there, & without giving his name asked if he could see Mr. Allan. She replied that Mr. Allan's condition was such that his physicians had prohibited any person from seeing him except his nurses. The man was Edgar A. Poe, who was, of course, perfectly familiar with the house. Thrusting her aside & without noticing her reply, he passed rapidly upstairs to Mr. Allan's chamber, followed by Mrs. Allan. As soon as he entered the chamber, Mr. Allan raised his cane, & threatening to strike him if he came within his reach, ordered him out.

Cursed instead of blessed by his father, and driven from the family home by the enraged old man, Poe passed out of Allan's life forever.

Allan once said that he rarely suffered unavailing regrets. Influenced by his kindly first wife, he had been affectionate, generous, even extravagant during Poe's childhood. But after their bitter quarrels and Allan's second marriage, he wrote Poe off, with few pangs of conscience, as a bad lot. When he died six weeks after Poe's rash visit, on March 27, 1834, Allan made good his threat to "turn him adrift" and left Poe absolutely nothing. Poe had been taught the habits and tastes of a gentle-man, but denied the means to support them.

Poe portrayed the methodical materialism of men like Allan in "The Business Man," in which the satiric victim expresses intense hostility to the artist: "If there is any thing on earth I hate, it is a genius. You geniuses are all arrant asses—the greater the genius, the greater the ass. . . . Especially, you cannot make a man of business out of a genius." The bitter lines from Yeats' "September 1913" express Poe's response to the philistine business mentality that ignored or despised his genius:

What need you, being come to sense,

But fumble in a greasy till

And add the halfpence to the pence

And prayer to shivering prayer, until

You have dried the marrow from the bone?

Unfortunately, Allan's tragic lack of forgiveness dried the marrow from Poe's bone as well as from his own.

Poe's Derangement in the Late 1840s

Scott Peeples

Scott Peeples, a professor of English at the College of Charleston, has written two books on Edgar Allan Poe and is coeditor of the journal Poe Studies.

In the following selection Peeples examines Poe's mental condition in the last years of his life, from 1845 to 1849. These were years marked by drunken rages, paranoia, and suicide attempts. His writings—especially the tales and the poem "The Raven"— had brought him recognition but not enough income to live on. While living in dire poverty, Virginia, his first cousin who had become his wife, became profoundly ill. Poe confessed to a friend, "I believe I have been mad." Certainly his behavior suggested this self-diagnosis. He became jealous of other writers, made petty public comments about others, and even engaged in physical brawls. One of his enemies claimed repeatedly and in public that Poe had been committed to a mental institution. The character of Montresor in "The Cask of Amontillado" is the self-portrait of a man with a quick mind but perverse heart who seeks revenge against an enemy who has "insulted" him.

Within months of "The Raven"'s publication, Poe became a desirable guest at New York literary salons, and in the summer of 1845 he formed a partnership that gave him a one-third financial interest in a weekly magazine, the *Broadway Journal*. He also published another collection of tales and his first volume of poetry in 14 years, *The Raven and Other Poems*.

Publication but No Money

But once again bad luck and self-destructive impulses over-whelmed Poe's hopes for lasting success. In the same letter in which he boasted of "The Raven"'s "great run," he complained: "I have made no money. I am as poor now as ever I was in my life—except in hope, which is by no means bankable". His financial bind would tighten, in fact, as the *Broadway Journal* soon turned into a money pit rather than a source of profit, folding just two months after he gained sole ownership. Mean-while, *Tales*, although well reviewed, earned him only $120, and he apparently made little or nothing from *The Raven and Other Poems*.

Had Poe maintained the creative energy that had seen him through hard times in Philadelphia—or had he really been able to manufacture popular literature as he claimed in "The Philosophy of Composition"—he might have built something "bankable" on the fame he won with "The Raven." But the combination of [his wife] Virginia's worsening condition, the demise of the *Journal*, bouts of paranoia, and a counterpro-ductive streak of professional jealousy overwhelmed him, trig-gering more debilitating drinking binges. During a lucid inter-val in November 1845, he told his friend Evert Duyckinck, "I really believe that I have been mad."

Social Disasters

A few incidents illustrate Poe's tendency during this period to alienate associates and worsen his personal reputation. In 1845 the Boston Lyceum, which organized popular public lectures, invited Poe to lead off their series in October. Poe accepted but, in the midst of writer's block and bouts of drinking and illness, found himself unable to compose a new poem. Rather than cancel or simply admit at the performance that he was reading already-published poems, he tried to pawn off his early long poem "Al Aaraaf" as a new work, now titled "The Messenger Star." Poe's audience, which had already heard a long speech before he came onstage, apparently responded unenthusiastically, and the crowd thinned before Poe closed with a reading of "The Raven." The performance received unfavorable reviews from the Boston press, not surprising since Poe had already declared himself hostile to the New England literary establishment in print and had repeatedly insulted [Henry Wadsworth] Longfellow, the city's most celebrated poet. But rather than cut his losses, Poe continued to bait his Bostonian audience and the city's editors. He not only revealed his deception but falsely claimed that he had written the poem before the age of 12, and that he had read a poem he acknowledged as inferior, inscrutable work to show his disdain for Bostonians. Once back in New York, he described the episode in the pages of the *Broadway Journal* as an ingenious hoax, but his attempts to save face or turn what should have been a small embarrassment into a triumph seem merely pathetic, symptomatic of his increasing combativeness and loss of perspective.

Earlier that year, while he was still the toast of the New York literary salons, Poe became acquainted with, and apparently charmed, a number of literary women, among them the popular poet Frances Osgood. Although it is unlikely that their relationship was sexual, Poe and Osgood flirted openly at literary gatherings and also visited and wrote each other frequently. When some of Osgood's friends persuaded her to reclaim her "indiscreet" letters, Poe reportedly told one of her emissaries, Elizabeth Ellet, that she should "look after her *own* letters," by implication letters to Poe himself. At that point Ellet's brother, William H. Lummis, demanded the return of Ellet's letters, which Poe claimed he had already given back. In his fear of Lummis, Poe sought the help of Thomas Dunn English, more often his enemy than his friend, asking English to lend him a pistol. English refused, Poe became irate, and the two men scuffled. Both later claimed victory, but youth, good health, and physical size were all on English's side. While recovering from this brawl, Poe avoided more serious violence by smoothing the matter over with a letter to Lummis in which he denied having referred to an indiscreet correspondence with Ellet and pleaded temporary insanity in case he *had* made such an accusation. Nevertheless, Poe had offended the polite society of literary New York, and he was now excluded from the salons where other influential writers and patrons of the arts mingled and made contacts. . . .

Virginia's Death

For the most part, Poe brought scandal on himself, but personal misery seemed to prey upon him at the same time. Five years after her first dramatic signs of tuberculosis, Virginia died in February of 1847. Poe, too, fell ill in late 1846 and early 1847, suffering from what more than one friend called a "brain fever"; he was probably malnourished and, along with Muddy [Virginia's mother, Maria Clemm,] and Virginia, had little protection against the harsh winter weather. At least partly to avoid the unhealthy environment of the city, Poe had moved the family to a small cottage in Fordham, about 13 miles from Manhattan, in May of 1846. But neither Virginia's health nor Poe's improved, and after her death his grief weakened him even more. . . .

In July 1848 Poe visited Jane Locke, a poet with whom he had exchanged several letters, in Lowell, Massachusetts, but discovered there that she was married. While in Lowell, Poe met Nancy Richmond, another married woman, whom he found much more appealing than Jane Locke. Poe and "Annie," as he called Mrs. Richmond, maintained a close friendship until his death, but Poe's letters to her make it clear that he wished they could marry. In November of 1848, driven at least partly by despair over Annie, Poe attempted suicide by taking an overdose of laudanum (opium dissolved in alcohol, legal and widely used in the nineteenth century). After swallowing an ounce (30 times the average dose), he wrote Annie

Virginia Poe, Edgar Allan Poe's first cousin and wife, died of tuberculosis. Her death aided in her husband's loss of perspective. © Mary Evans Picture Library/Alamy.

asking her to come to him, with the plan of taking another ounce when she arrived, but in his stupor he failed to mail the letter and probably came close to dying over the next two days.

Although Poe never abandoned his dream of a marriage to Annie, by the time he attempted suicide he was in the midst of another ill-fated romance. Sarah Helen Whitman, a poet from a well-to-do Providence family, greatly admired Poe and seriously considered marrying him. But Whitman's mother disapproved, and friends warned her of Poe's instability. Worried by Poe's reputation and his drinking, she hesitated and placed conditions on their engagement; angered and hurt, Poe wrote her letters that were at once reprimands and pleas for love, similar in this regard to the letters he had written [his foster father] John Allan 20 years earlier. His behavior as well as his letters betrayed his instability, and by the time the newspapers announced their upcoming marriage in January 1849, Poe and Helen Whitman had broken off the engagement.

While Poe was desperately seeking a replacement for Virginia, he was also chasing another dream, that of controlling his own magazine. He had entered into a partnership with a prosperous and admiring young editor and publisher, E. H. N. Patterson, who agreed to help finance the magazine while giving Poe editorial control. Poe planned to tour the South and West, raising money with lectures and enlisting 1,000 subscribers, although as usual he would fall far short of his expectations. Poe began his "tour" on June 29, 1849, traveling first to Philadelphia. A cholera epidemic had broken out there, and Poe, if his account can be believed, became sick and took calomel, which contains mercury, to fight the disease. As a result of either mercury poisoning or a drinking binge—perhaps both—Poe became "deranged" for "more than ten days," according to his own report. He suffered hallucinations and became paranoid, but two friends, the engraver and magazine publisher John Sartin and novelist George Lippard, saw him through it and raised enough money to send him farther south.

Poe traveled on to Richmond, where he resumed his search for a wife, in this case the former Elmira Royster, whom he had courted as a teenager. Elmira's husband, Alexander Shelton, a successful businessman, had passed away five years earlier. Mrs. Shelton was impressed with Poe's literary accomplishments, and she was lonely since her husband's death; nostalgia and the promise of stability—emotional and financial—undoubtedly attracted Poe to her. But, like Helen Whitman, Elmira was wary of Poe's declarations of love, especially after so many years of estrangement, and she almost certainly knew that he had a drinking problem. Their marriage would have presented other difficulties as well: Elmira had two children, a responsibility for which Poe was unprepared, and she would lose much of her inheritance (to her 10-year-old son) once she married, in accordance with her husband's will. Mrs. Shelton later claimed that they had never really been engaged; for his part, Poe seems to have pursued the engagement although he harbored serious doubts. He wrote to Muddy that he believed the wedding would take place but also confessed to her "that my heart sinks at the idea of this marriage." Anticipating a marriage he did not really want, and still hoping that Patterson would finance his magazine, Poe left Richmond on the morning of September 27 on a steamship bound for Baltimore, the first scheduled stop on his journey home. He died there under mysterious circumstances 10 days later. . . .

Poe and Montresor as Mad Avengers

In "The Cask of Amontillado" (1846), one of Poe's most tightly constructed tales, the narrator takes revenge on both his adversarial double and on himself. Many critics have noted the story's biographical resonance for a writer who believed himself beset by a "thousand injuries" at the hands of various enemies and, at the very time he was writing the story, the insults of Thomas Dunn English. But along with the story's wish-fulfillment of silencing one's nemesis once and for all is Poe's continued awareness of the "circularity of revenge."

Irony pervades, even structures, the story. Although Poe immerses us in the perspective of the avenger Montresor, he discourages sympathy with him. Montresor claims to have been injured and insulted by Fortunato, but he never names Fortunato's specific offense. Moreover, the victim seems unaware of having offended Montresor. Even though Fortunato is drunk and wishes to prove his wine-tasting expertise, his lighthearted willingness to visit the catacombs of Montresor's mansion would be impossible if he had knowingly insulted his host "with impunity." The closest thing to a motive that emerges throughout their conversation is simple jealousy, for, as Montresor feigns concern for his victim's health, he tells him: "You are rich, respected, admired, beloved; you are happy, as once I was. You are a man to be missed. For me it is no matter". Montresor proves himself adept at duping other people, but he seems to have fooled himself into thinking he had a legitimate score to settle with Fortunato; more likely, he has "created" an enemy on whom he can blame his disappointments and failures.

More particular instances of irony fill Montresor's narrative; his use of language and psychology is so playful that if one does not take the story too seriously one can easily find him a likable murderer. He uses the same reverse psychology on his servants that he is using on Fortunato; to ensure their absence, he "told them that I should not return until the morning, and had given them explicit orders not to stir from the house". Conversely, while repeatedly urging Fortunato to leave, he ensures that he will stay simply by invoking the name of Luchesi, Fortunato's rival in wine connoisseurship. When Fortunato insists that they go on because, after all, he "shall not die of a cough," the man who knows precisely how he will die replies, "True—true". Not long afterward, Montresor answers Fortunato's toast "to the buried that repose around us" by drinking "to your long life". Even the choice of wine he offers Fortunato, "De Grave," puns on their destination, which will prove to be Fortunato's grave. . . . This exercise in taunting his unsuspecting victim (appropriately dressed in motley) peaks when Montresor shows Fortunato the trowel with which he will entomb him. Having tested Montresor by using a secret sign, Fortunato concludes that his friend is "not of the brotherhood." Montresor replies:

"How?"

"You are not of the masons."

"Yes, yes," I said, "yes, yes."

"You? Impossible! A mason?"

"A mason," I replied.

"A sign," he said.

"It is this," I answered, producing a trowel from beneath the folds of my *roquelaire.*

At this point one might expect Fortunato to ask why his friend is carrying around a trowel, but he is only shrewd enough to recognize the pun: "'You jest,' he exclaimed, recoiling a few paces. 'But let us proceed to the Amontillado'".

Fortunato proceeds, of course, to a slow and torturous death at the story's end, which brings us, as it so often does with Poe, back to the beginning, to Montresor's criteria for revenge: "*At length* I would be avenged; this was a point definitively settled—but the very definitiveness with which it was resolved precluded the idea of risk. I must not only punish, but punish with impunity. A wrong is unredressed when retribution overtakes its redresser. It is equally unredressed when the avenger fails to make himself felt as such to him who has done the wrong". At first glance Montresor would seem to have fulfilled both requirements: Fortunato cannot strike back, and he knows who has killed him. And yet Fortunato still does not seem to know that this is an act of revenge; Montresor apparently has "fail[ed] to make himself felt as such," that is, as an avenger. Furthermore, as most (though not all) commentators on this story assert, Montresor fails to fulfill the other criterion for true revenge, for the narrative itself is subtle evidence that retribution has overtaken him in the form of guilt. Fifty years later, he still remembers his heart's "growing sick—on account of the dampness of the catacombs," but this heartsickness likely arises from empathy with the man he is leaving to die amid that dampness. Montresor addresses his narrative to "[y]ou, who so well know the nature of my soul"—certainly not the reader, but, given Montresor's advanced age, very likely a priest or other confidante to whom he is making a deathbed confession. . . .

"The Cask of Amontillado," . . . can be read as Poe's fictional wish-fulfillment, for until the end of his life he continued to feel victimized by his enemies.

Social Issues in Literature

CHAPTER 2

Social and Psychological Disorder in Poe's Works

Poe's Characters as Self-Portraits

Claudia C. Morrison

Claudia C. Morrison, who has written widely on Edgar Allan Poe, is chiefly known for Freud and the Critic: The Early Use of Depth Psychology in Literary Criticism.

Morrison, in the following selection, raises the question about Poe's personal connection to the narrators of his stories and poems. Are they and he one and the same? She discusses, as an example, "Ligeia," in which a dead wife returns in the body of another woman. Here Poe reveals a deeper psychological plane than even he realized. His preoccupation with death and burial in "Ligeia" and other stories reveal Poe's longing for the return of his mother who died when he was two. "Ligeia" reveals Poe's belief that his mother's love for her son will be great enough to allow her to win the fight to return to him. Poe's obsession with the eyes of Ligeia parallels his memory of his mother's dying face. Even though these mothers have the will to return, the psychological connection between mother and son produces dread and horror.

The many and varied interpretations of Poe's "Ligeia" can be generally divided into two categories: those interpretations that examine the tale as a consciously contrived story of the supernatural with, possibly, allegorical overtones; and those that emphasize the psychological aspects of "Ligeia" and treat it as a revelation of conflicts within Poe's own personality, or those of the "narrator" of the tale. Regarding the latter interpretations, [critic] David M. Rein saw in it evidence of Poe's unconscious hostility toward Virginia Clemm [Poe's

Claudia C. Morrison, "Poe's 'Ligeia': An Analysis," *Studies in Short Fiction*, vol. 4, Spring 1967, pp. 234–42. Copyright © 1967 by Studies in Short Fiction. Reproduced by permission.

wife] who appears in the story disguised as the figure of Rowena; and Marie Bonaparte has presented a lengthy psychoanalytic analysis of the story as an unconscious portrayal of Poe's repressed sado-masochistic desire for dead [mother,] Elizabeth Arnold Poe.

Psychological Interpretations

Several of the psychological critics of the tale have suggested that it contains an allegorical expression of the "impossibility of finding a substitute for a first love, when that love is obsessive; and the obliteration of the substitute in the lover's yearning memory of the first love," without identifying biographically this "obsessive" first love in Poe's life. Still other psychological interpreters of *Ligeia* avoid biographical inferences altogether and treat the story as a consciously elaborated fiction of a madman's megalomaniac obsession, insisting that Poe the author is not to be identified with the fictional narrator of the drama. "I believe," writes James W. Gargano, "that 'Ligeia' can best be understood as the tale of a man (the narrator and not Poe) who, having once inhabited the realm of the Ideal, seeks even unto madness to recreate a lost ecstasy."

The most prominent of those who insist that the dramatized narrator is not to be confused with Poe himself is Roy P. Basler, who in his book *Sex, Symbolism and Psychology in Literature* put forward an interpretation of "Ligeia" which concluded that the crazed narrator, a megalomaniac and a psychopath, murders Rowena and hallucinates Ligeia's return. This interpretation has been thoroughly refuted by James Schroeter in an excellent article in *PMLA* [*Publications of the Modern Language Association*], wherein Schroeter pointed out that Poe himself did not object to being identified with his "narrator". . . .

It is the thesis of this paper that at least part of the emotional impact of "Ligeia" is due to elements in the theme of the story of which both Poe and his readers were largely unconscious, and that the "almost obscene overwriting" of parts of the tale is the result of a deeper psychological investment in the narrative situation of "Ligeia" than the author was consciously aware of.

The Dead Mother

Depth psychology, particularly Freudian psychology, has contributed many provocative hypotheses about the psychological development of the child, and post-Freudian investigators have added a wealth of information about the nature of the child's thought processes. Some of this information is highly relevant to Poe's stories if we can accept the premise that Poe's repeated use of death, graves, and corpses as thematic material for his stories and poems represents something more than a calculated aim to manipulate popular interest in the Gothic. It is difficult to conceive that Poe's concept that the theme of greatest beauty was the death of a beautiful woman is unrelated to the facts of his life experience, which included not only the early deaths of his mother and his wife but of several other love objects as well. . . . The frequent repetition of the agonizing loss of women with whom he had developed strong emotional ties would predispose any human being to a certain preoccupation with death; and in the case of a man like Poe, who witnessed the long, drawn-out tubercular illness and death of his mother shortly before his third birthday, it would serve to reinforce what is generally accepted by most psychologists to be a major traumatic occurrence for any child. Viewing Poe's life and art through a psychological lens, one cannot fail to see in such a story as "Ligeia" a sophisticated structuring of an unconscious wish for the return of Poe's lost mother. Before examining the story in these terms, however, it would be helpful to review some of the insights that contemporary child psychology has offered into the nature of the child's response to death.

Edgar Allan Poe's short story Ligeia *draws a parallel to his personal experience with his wife's death. In the film* The Tomb of Ligeia, *Verden Fell's (Vincent Price) obsession with and desire for the return of his dead wife, Ligeia (Elizabeth Shepherd), causes problems in his second marriage with Rowena Trevanion (also played by Shepherd).* © Photos 12/ Alamy.

The Child and Death

Death is difficult for an adult mind to conceive, but it is even harder for the child, who tends to be far more literal and concrete in his thinking than the adult and has a correspondingly greater difficulty handling abstractions. When someone in the child's world dies, the only experience with which he can analogize the situation and make it comprehensible is the familiar disappearance and reappearance of people whom he knows. The concept that someone—a person or an animal—has gone away permanently is normally met with disbelief on the part of the child and with the certainty that the person will reappear within a short time. Another common belief that further complicates the young child's initial inability to comprehend death is the childish faith in the omnipotence of adults, particularly parents. Almost anyone who has associated with children before the age of three has had the frustrating experience of attempting to convince the child that such-and-such activity is really beyond the adult's powers—that the parent really can't make it stop raining or that he can't produce a certain television program on Thursday that appears only on Saturday. Only gradually does the child come to accept the idea that parents are limited and finite, and that they do not govern the immediate universe by the force of their wills. It is not surprising, then, for the two-year-old child to believe that the death of a parent is a *willed* disappearance, and that if the parent really desired to do so, he could return. In the child's view, the parent has abandoned him for some cause, usually one, he reasons, that is in some way connected with his own behavior. Much childish anxiety and guilt in the face of the death of a parent can be traced back to this reasoning process, for the child tends to assume that he must be responsible for the parent's leaving him and depriving him of maternal (or paternal) love and protection. The reverse of this concept would also follow logically: if the parent has left because the child has been "bad," then if the child is "good," or if the parent loved him enough in spite of his "badness," the parent will reappear—a logic that appears quite reasonable once one grasps the child's firm belief in his fundamental premise, that of parental omnipotence.

Poe's Mother's Eyes

If we apply these concepts of the child's thought patterns to an examination of "Ligeia," it is possible to see the unconscious germ of the story as having originated in Poe's feelings concerning the loss of his mother, Elizabeth Arnold Poe, who died at age twenty-four. Poe's own statements of the origin of the idea for "Ligeia" are in accord with this hypothesis. On the copy of the *Broadway Journal* which Poe sent to [his friend] Mrs. [Sarah Helen] Whitman in 1845, he wrote, "The poem ["To Helen," 1848] which I sent you contained all the events of a *dream* which occurred to me soon after I knew you. Ligeia was also suggested by a *dream*—observe the *eyes* in both tale and poem." The relevant lines in "To Helen" are these:

All—all expired save thee—save less than thou:

Save only the divine light in thine eyes—

Save but the soul in thine uplifted eyes.

I saw but them—they were the world to me.

I saw but them—saw only them for hours—

Saw only them until the moon went down.

What wild heart-histories seemed to lie en-written

Upon those crystalline, celestial spheres!

How dark a wo! yet how sublime a hope!

How silently serene a sea of pride!

How daring an ambition! yet how deep—

How fathomless a capacity for love!

In reading these lines, one cannot help but be struck by the fact that Poe as a child was present in the room when his mother died; it would seem that the staring eyes, either of his dying tubercular mother, or of her corpse, or both, made a deep impression on the young boy. It is as if the memory of the child's emotional experience of witnessing the death of his parent has been translated into the poem, idealized, of course, and put into a particular dramatic setting—for the memory of Elizabeth Arnold's death was not a conscious one. That the germ of both "To Helen" and "Ligeia" was an unconscious memory is testified to by the fact that Poe experienced these eyes in a dream, a dream of such emotional intensity and personal meaning that he felt compelled to embody the experience twice in works of literature, perhaps in an effort to comprehend its significance. It was the mystery connected with the meaning of the eyes in the dream that Poe emphasizes in the story, where it becomes the narrator's almost obsessed desire to fathom the significance of the *expression* of the eyes of Ligeia. Poe devoted an entire paragraph to a description of these eyes, and the paragraph is so arranged as to be the climax of the portrait of this remarkable woman who is portrayed as having the attributes of a goddess. The paragraph concludes:

> The "strangeness," however, which I found in the eyes was of a nature distinct from the formation, or the color, or the brilliancy of the features, and must, after all, be referred to the *expression*. Ah, word of no meaning! behind whose vast latitude of mere sound we intrench our ignorance of so much of the spiritual. The expression of the eyes of Ligeia! How for long hours have I pondered upon it! How have I, through the whole of a mid-summer night, struggled to fathom it! What was it—that something more profound

than the well of Democritus—which lay far within the pupils of my beloved. What *was* it? I was possessed with a passion to discover. Those eyes! those large, those shining, those divine orbs! they became to me twin stars of Leda, and I to them devoutest of astrologers. . . .

Mother and Son

The symbolism of the eyes remains unknown to the narrator, but he begins to experience the same effect associated with them when in the presence of various objects in Nature. In the catalogue of these objects, which includes a growing vine, a butterfly, a stream, the ocean, a meteor, it is interesting that the climactic object to which the narrator transfers this emotion is the "quotation" from Glanville about the supremacy of the will. This is the first occurrence of this crucial passage in the tale (except for the headnote) and if, as I have tried to suggest, the eyes of Poe's dream are indeed the eyes of Poe's lost mother, the latent content of dream and story is the fantasy that the omnipotent parent, through her overwhelming love of her child, can will herself to return to him.

It has been several times pointed out that in his description of Ligeia, Poe places himself (or, rather, the narrator) in relation to Ligeia as a child to his mother. The narrator's adoration, even idolatry, for Ligeia has struck many critics as excessive, and the sum total of her perfections does seem to violate any canon of probability. Seen as an unconscious reflection of the child's overestimation of his parent, however, the description makes excellent psychological sense. Ligeia is described as being tall—as all adults appear to the child's mind; her beauty recalls the "fabulous Houri of the Turk"; and her mental powers are described as "immense"—one is reminded that to the child, the parent appears to be omniscient. Like a small boy, the narrator resigns himself "with a childlike confidence" to the "infinite supremacy" of Ligeia's teachings, and as she "bends over him in studies but little sought" he feels as if he "might at length pass onward to the goal of a wisdom too divinely precious not to be forbidden". Without her guidance, he is "but a child groping benighted." It is not until she becomes possessed of a mysterious disease which finally kills her that the narrator understands the intensity of her love for him, a "more than womanly abandonment to a love, alas! all unmerited," which is the reason she struggles so fiercely against death. After having the narrator read to her "The Conqueror Worm," a poem expressing the concepts of fate and determinism, Ligeia dies, twice repudiating this doctrine and "half-shrieking" her refusal (and, unconsciously, Poe's) to accept the finality of death and the separation from the man she loves: "Man doth not yield him to the angels nor unto death utterly save only through the weakness of his feeble will."

The Mother's Return

The second half of "Ligeia" involves the actual realization of this fantasy—the fulfillment of the wish that the loved woman shall return. The narrator, with no other motive than "a moment of mental alienation," marries the Lady Rowena Trevanion, a marriage which is briefly described as "unhallowed." His sense of betrayal to his love for his first wife leads to a loathing for his bride that aggravates the mysterious illness to which she shortly succumbs. The remainder of the narrative relates the dramatic struggles and relapses of the dead Rowena that the narrator observes with intense excitement. Poe skillfully handles the drama in this second half of the story and builds to the climax of the final lines when the successful possession of Rowena's corpse by the dead Ligeia is fully revealed to the narrator, who shrieks aloud with an emotion compounded half of wonder, half of terror: "Here then, at least, can I never—can I never be mistaken—these are the full, and the black, and the wild eyes—of my lost love—of the Lady—of the Lady Ligeia". The fantasy is complete; the meaning of the expression of the eyes, which at the same time "so delighted and appalled" the narrator, has been revealed, and the narrator-Poe is at last possessed of the lost love who through the force of her "gigantic" will has returned to him. Through her omnipotence, the mother has returned to the once-abandoned child.

But if the underlying, latent content of "Ligeia" is rooted in the child's fantasy that the dead mother can return to him through the strength of her love and the force of her will, how is one to explain the predominant tone of dread and anxiety present in the tale? It is possible to account for the dominant affective response to "Ligeia" on the basis of the fact that the subject matter of the return of the dead is simply a fear-arousing subject, and that Poe was counting on this universal response in constructing his tale, which is, after all, a Gothic horror story.

Madness as Realism, Not Supernaturalism

Vincent Buranelli

Vincent Buranelli is the author of books for both adults and children, including several books in the Hardy Boys series, and rewrote many classic works for young readers.

Buranelli points out in the following excerpt that Edgar Allan Poe's horror stories are rooted in reality, not supernaturalism. His gothic stories are made horrible—not by vampires, angels, and werewolves—but by psychological perversions. Nor are the centers of the tales moral or ethical, though sometimes bad people come to bad ends. His murderous narrators are not to be blamed, because they are the victims of psychological abnormalities, including hallucinations, neuroses, and psychoses; they should be in mental institutions, not on the gallows. The narrators of Poe's tales begin their stories long after their manias have developed, so when we meet them, their madness has gone too far for them to understand or control events. Such stories as "Berenice," "The Black Cat," "The Tell-Tale Heart" and "The Cask of Amontillado" are not dark fantasy but stark realism—as anyone who reads the daily newspapers can see.

If there is more in Poe's artistic universe than horror and terror, these are, as far as his short stories are concerned, the characteristics that seem most prominent and have attracted most attention. His humor and hoaxes, his satire and fantasies, are pallid compared to the throbbing energy of his gruesome and frightening themes. He took a literary genre with a very high mortality rate—the Gothic tale—and trans-

Vincent Buranelli, *Edgar Allan Poe*. Boston: Twayne Publishers, 1977. Copyright © 1977 by G.K. Hall & Co. All rights reserved. Reproduced by permission of Gale, a part of Cengage Learning.

formed it into something alive and lasting. . . . Who has not read "The Tell-Tale Heart," "The Pit and the Pendulum," "The Fall of the House of Usher"?

Poe's scope is narrow, but he has remarkable success in avoiding monotony by subtly varying the treatment of stories that resemble one another. He cannot paint his characters fully. According to his stated principle, he does not have to since the unveiling of character is the function of the novel. On the other hand, while his women are much alike (each is his ideal woman in whom traces of his mother and his wife may be found), his men reveal marked differences even in quite brief introductions. William Wilson in flight from himself could not be mistaken for the crazed narrator of "The Black Cat," or paranoic Metzengerstein for Montresor, the sly sadist of "The Cask of Amontillado."

Poe's narrowness is like that of a sword, not that of a bottleneck: it is effective rather than constricting. Nothing adventitious is in his great stories, only the essentials, the minimum of characterization, plot, and atmosphere. By ridding himself of everything except what is precisely to the point, he achieves his unity of effect.

Not Morality but Psychology

Poe, by deliberate choice, is not a moralist in his fiction. Morality can be found in the tales; for, as he has himself told us, goodness and truth are by-products of art. Since words loaded with ethical content are scattered through his pages—"evil," "wickedness," "vice," "turpitude," "dissipation," "profligacy," "debauchery," "cruelty"—a distinction between right and wrong is implied. Moreover, vicious characters tend to come to a bad end. In "Metzengerstein," pride has a fall; in "The Masque of the Red Death," an attempt to hide from a suffering world leads back to it; in "Hop-Frog," brutality is punished. The reader may accept these endings as a triumph of good over evil. Nothing in the stories forbids him to do so: they are neither immoral nor amoral.

Poe writes, nevertheless, from the standpoint of psychology rather than ethics. It is nearly impossible to condemn sin and crime in Poe's universe as vices that spring from the rational will of a responsible human being. The terrible deeds that abound there result from the pressures of abnormal psychology—from neurasthenia, hallucinations, neuroses, and psychoses. Remorse is always a compulsion, never the self-accusation of a stable conscience after a free and deliberate act. Poe's characters are so far from normality that none should be forced to plead to an indictment in a court of law. The narrator of "The Black Cat" will stand on the gallows, but we know that he should be in an asylum for the criminally insane. William Wilson is haunted by his conscience, but this story is a doppelgänger drama—about the terrifying double of oneself so popular in German literature—rather than a morality play. While "The Pit and the Pendulum" sees the Inquisition defeated, the real ending is the victim's escape after all his agonies and terrors....

Blending the Natural and the Weird

In his Gothic fiction, Poe handles the morbid and frightening subjects with which his reputation is so closely associated—death, madness, disease, the dissolution of personality, the wasting away of fragile heroines. Sometimes the incidents recounted are realistic: "The Assignation" tells of suicide in luxurious apartments above the moonlit lagoon of Venice; "The Oblong Box" is about a man driven out of his mind by grief and clinging to the corpse of his dead wife. At other times the uncanny creeps in: "Metzengerstein" features a spectral horse; "MS. Found in a Bottle," a ghostly ship; and "The Masque of the Red Death" is an allegory in which Death is one of the *dramatis personae*. Yet again, Poe's habit is to blend the natural and the weird by postulating hidden but rational laws that govern the action. In "The Oval Portrait," by some occult process the act of painting draws life from the sitter and transfers it to her image. In "The Fall of the House of Usher," the tragedy is so far from being either gratuitous or a matter of capricious volition that both family and mansion are foredoomed to destruction. . . .

Dissolution of the Personality

Mystery is related to psychology in Poe's works. He finds the interplay of the parts of the soul a subject that can be invested with weird overtones [if] the faculties are seen, not as cooperating in the normal way, but as involved in a turbulent psychological civil war. One of his key thoughts concerning this topic is about the dissolution of personality. "The Imp of the Perverse" describes a tyrannous impulse warring on the rest of the soul, compelling it to do what the other faculties say should not be done. The protagonist of "The Man of the Crowd" is anxious to join in human fellowship, and unable to do so for some contrary and overriding motive buried in the depths of his psyche. He is almost a foreshadowing of the individual dehumanized and lost in the mass, of whom twentieth-century authors have written so frequently.

The finest thing Poe ever did along these lines is "William Wilson." This is a man's struggle with his conscience, which is allegorized, objectified in another man of the same name and appearance. William Wilson, who meets his conscience first at school, spends the rest of his life trying to evade it. Wherever he goes, whatever he does (and he does some very vicious things), his counterpart inevitably catches up with, and exposes, him. This "spectre" pursues him from school to Oxford, Paris, Vienna, Berlin, Moscow. Finally, during carnival time in Rome, William Wilson turns upon his tormentor. He corners the second William Wilson, stabs him to death—and realizes too late that he has murdered his own conscience, and therefore ruined himself. . . .

Obsessive Murders

The dissolution of personality theme cuts into complicated psychology. Elsewhere Poe studies the mind, not when it suffers from an anarchy of its faculties, but when it is under the tyranny of some one element, one idea or obsession. He enters the field of the starkly, almost clinically, realistic investigation of men who, although they may feel uneasy about their mental states when their tension lets up, are too far gone to understand their mania, let alone to control it.

"Berenice" set the pattern for the later stories of the same type. Egaeus commits the hideous act of opening the grave of Berenice and pulling out her teeth. Yet he knows nothing about it since he is in a state of shock and trance at the time. Since Berenice is said to have been buried alive and therefore to have been the victim of a ghoulish mayhem, Poe was criticized for attacking such a subject; and he admitted, possibly only half in earnest, that he too considered that he had been excessive in trying for a shock-reaction among his readers. He promised to stay within bounds, and did so with "The Tell-Tale Heart" and "The Black Cat."

Each of these has a horrible obsessive murder for its theme, and each follows the development of the theme step by step with a realism that, barring the writing genius, might be a case history from twentieth-century psychiatry. Those who deny realism to Poe cannot be very familiar with our daily newspapers, which periodically carry true stories of murders committed under just such abnormal psychological pressures as those described in "The Tell-Tale Heart" and "The Black Cat."

These two stories demonstrate how varied Poe can be within narrow limits. The former is a direct account by a maniac of how he committed murder because of a delusive compulsion, carefully concealed the crime, and then was driven by a further thrust of his compulsion to reveal it to the police. "The Black Cat" portrays a maniac wavering in his attitudes, killing his wife in one insane paroxysm, when what he really hates is his cat, and causing the truth to come to light by an insane act of bravado. The first murderer seats the police over the grave of his victim, and is exposed only because his rising mania makes him give himself away. The second murderer taunts the police by rapping on the wall where his wife is buried, and is exposed by the wail of the cat that he has inadvertently walled up with her. . . .

Montresor, the Mad Perfectionist

Poe's gem of realism—not his best story because its dimensions are too small, but perfect within its format—is "The Cask of Amontillado." Finely-wrought, tight, neat, with no loose ends or superfluities, it strikes with tremendous force within the space of some five pages. Since Montresor is without a conscience, there are no doubts, hesitations or second thoughts to impede the narrative. We do not even know his motive, nor do we need to. It is sufficient that, committed to revenge, and to a certain kind of revenge, he, with the frigid intelligence of an Iago [villain in Shakespeare's *Othello*], with the open-faced cunning of a confidence man, entices Fortunato into the vaults, chains him to a wall, and proceeds to entomb him alive. The brutal directness of the treatment reminds us of the *verismo* [realism] that Ernest Hemingway brought to his celebrated short story "The Killers." On the other hand, "Hop Frog," another story of revenge, has no such realism: It is laid in a Gothic court, and the revenge of the hunchback on King and courtiers in a body is too excessive to be believed. . . .

Poe's Creation of Mental States

There are two peculiarly arresting attributes in Poe's short stories—atmosphere and the description of mental states. The tricks of creating atmosphere he largely derived from the tradition of the Gothic tale: He pruned and tightened and in

Edgar Allan Poe's horror stories, including The Pit and the Pendulum, *are rooted in reality and made horrific by psychological perversions.* © Lebrecht Music and Arts Photo Library/ Alamy.

part augmented what he found in earlier writers. But the description of mental states is virtually his own creation, something he worked out by consulting his own psychology. That is the secret of his understanding. His ability to put this understanding to work in literature is the mystery of his genius.

No one has ever surpassed him, and few have ever equalled him, when it comes to an analysis of emotion washing across the soul like the ebb and flow of the tide. There is an undulation of terror in the soul of William Wilson, Roderick Usher, and the prisoner of "The Pit and the Pendulum." Obsessive fury rises, falls, and rises again, mounting to a crescendo, in the deranged brains of the homicidal maniacs of "The Tell-Tale Heart" and "The Black Cat." When Ligeia returns from the dead to seize upon the remains of her successor, the reincarnation takes place after a series of quivering palpitations in the corpse, after a series of nervous shocks suffered by the husband. . . .

Of the best of Poe there can be no question. Reading his greatest horror stories is an experience that anyone would be the poorer without, for Poe has constructed a universe to which there is nothing comparable in any literature. He has not cast his net widely over reality, but he *has* cast it deeply, and it *does* plumb reality.

Edgar Allan Poe and the Insanity Plea

John Cleman

John Cleman teaches at California State University, Los Angeles, and is a specialist in nineteenth-century fiction writers. He has written on Edgar Allan Poe and early American novelists George Washington Cable and Charles Brockton Brown.

In the following essay Cleman examines the conclusion reached by many critics that Poe has little or no interest in morality but focuses solely on the abnormal state of his characters. To arrive at his own argument, Cleman begins by examining the insanity defense of the courts in the nineteenth century. Two cases of the insanity defense were in the public eye when Poe was writing "The Black Cat," "The Tell-Tale Heart," and "The Imp of the Perverse," stories in which the narrators' sanity is at issue. Some narrators are seemingly unaware of their insanity even as they reveal it, and others offer their madness as a means of avoiding responsibility. By stressing the gruesomeness of the crimes, Poe undermines the insanity defense.

Poe's fascination with stories of crime, sometimes gleaned from contemporary newspaper accounts, is obvious enough from such examples as "The Oblong Box" (1844), "The Mystery of Marie Rogêt" (1842–43), and "The Murders in the Rue Morgue" (1841). In these and similar tales Poe's interest centers on the processes of detection, leaving the moral issues of the crimes either largely unaddressed or curiously deflected. . . .

John Cleman, "Irresistible Impulses: Edgar Allan Poe and the Insanity Defense," *American Literature*, vol. 63, December 1991, pp. 623–26, 630–37, 640. Copyright © 1991, Duke University Press. All rights reserved. Used by permission of the publisher.

A Moral Anarchy

Apart from the aesthetic, Poe's emphasis is usually read to center in the psychological or in the exercise of an individual will acting as a microcosm of the Universal Will. Edward Davidson, for example, observes that "Poe removed all moral and religious considerations as far as possible from any social code or body of religious warrants." Operating in a universe in which there is "no other god but the self as god," each of the characters "in Poe's moral inquiries is his own moral arbiter, lodged in a total moral anarchy. Society has invented law and justice, but these are mere illusion and exact no true penalty."

Reform in Treatment of the Insane

In England, the controversy over the increased use of the insanity defense in the first half of the nineteenth century, was stimulated by a number of factors. The political nature of the most celebrated cases, especially that of Daniel McNaughton in 1843, argued to many that the defense was undermining civil order. In addition, asylum reform and the increased popularity of what was known as "moral treatment" of the insane certainly contributed to the public perception that to be acquitted on the basis of insanity was to avoid punishment. . . .

Poe's familiarity with the scientific/medical accounts of insanity of his day has been well established, and his awareness of the issues of the insanity-defense controversy can be linked to two specific cases in which the defense was employed, both occurring in the environs of Philadelphia where Poe resided between 1838 and 1844, and both featuring the same attorney, Peter A. Browne, who [according to a 1843 *New York Herald* account] "had distinguished himself . . . for his great subtilty and deep metaphysical research in the matter of *insanity*." In the first of these, James Wood was acquitted on the grounds of insanity of the deliberate murder of his daughter. Lengthy accounts of the trial appeared daily in the Philadelphia *Public*

Ledger from 24 to 30 March 1840, and a comment at its conclusion appearing in the 1 April 1840 issue of *Alexander's Weekly Messenger* has been attributed to Poe.

The second case, the trial of Singleton Mercer, while less directly linked to Poe, signals more clearly the terms of the insanity-defense controversy. Mercer was charged with murdering his sister's seducer in February 1843. Both Mercer and his victim were well-known "men about town" in Philadelphia, and the Philadelphia and New York newspapers carried daily accounts of the court's proceedings, loaded with sensational details of sex, violence, and public corruption. . . .

Mysterious Physical Forces

The insanity-defense arguments of the mid-nineteenth century—those such as Browne's which helped provoke the controversy—posited a view of human nature ruled not by reasoned choice but by chance and ultimately mysterious physical forces. Not only was the boundary between the rational and irrational blurred, often wearing the same mask, the grounds for moral responsibility shifted as well. As Browne observed, courts and the public were asked to change their opinion "as to [the] *real nature of actions*, which are either *atrocious crimes*, or the *dreadful effects of disease*." The signalling feature to effect this shift from condemnation to pity was an inexplicable compulsion, an impelling force potential in everyone.

Of the three tales we are considering, "The Tell-Tale Heart" presents the most apparent evidence of Poe's use of the issues of the insanity defense. The characteristic form of all three tales is not confession but self-defense, an attempt to provide a rational account of apparently irrational events and behavior. In "The Tell-Tale Heart" there is a good deal of dramatic immediacy to this defense. The narrator addresses a specific but unnamed "you" sometime after his arrest but obviously before his execution (if there is to be one). His aim is to refute "you"'s claim that he is insane, a charge that has appar-

An illustration of Edgar Allan Poe's The Tell-Tale Heart. © Mary Evans Picture Library/
The Image Works.

ently been both specific and formal enough for the narrator
to feel the necessity of responding in earnest and in detail.
From the abrupt opening ("True!—nervous—very, very dread-
fully nervous I had been and am: but why *will* you say that I
am mad?") to the final dramatic breakdown ("and now—

again!—hark! louder! louder! louder! *louder!*") the narration seems more spoken than written, something like a courtroom outburst or final statement of the accused.

The point of suggesting such a context for the tale's telling is to underscore a particular significance of the narrator's insistence on his own sanity. The argument he offers reflects the issues of the insanity-defense controversy, both in the way he measures his own state of mind and in the type of madman he reveals himself to be. His argument echoes the terms by which an eighteenth-century prosecutor, employing the "wild beast" test of insanity, might have differentiated the accused (himself) from the recognizably nonculpable madman. Such madmen, according to the narrator, are mentally defective ("Madmen know nothing"), physically impaired ("senses . . . destroyed . . . dulled"), incapable of wisdom or "sagacity" in planning, at the mercy of impulse and passion. He, on the other hand, exhibited unmistakable signs of rational behavior in the way he carried out his crime: note, he repeatedly insists, "how wisely I proceeded—with what caution—with what foresight." He also asks the auditor to "observe how healthily—how calmly" he "can tell you the whole story." Thus, insofar as the narrator is manifestly not a "wild beast," the "prosecutor's argument" succeeds: the narrator is capable of reason and is, therefore, morally and legally responsible for his acts.

Of course, in telling his tale, particularly if imagined as a statement in court, the narrator is also offering clear evidence that he is by contemporary standards partially insane. Like the many monomaniacs Browne describes, the narrator has a highly developed intellect, is capable of planning and remembering his actions in great detail, but his intellect and energies are fixed unreasonably on a single goal or "one dominant idea" (the old man's "vulture eye") "that rides rough-shod over his brain—that haunts him day and night until it is granted." . . .

Even the narrator's insistent denial of the charge of insanity fits the pattern of symptoms of the homicidal maniac, so that the act of the tale's telling and its self-defensive posture constitute evidence in a determination of partial insanity. . . .

Pretending Insanity?

Poe's interest in the "cunning of the maniac" in simulating "perfect sanity" has more than clinical or literary significance: properly recognized it may convict the accused of insanity, but it thereby acquits him of murder and offers the possibility of his ultimate release to murder again.

In "The Tell-Tale Heart" the outcome is less certain, but the same concerns seem to apply. If the narrator demonstrates his own insanity . . . then the telling of the tale would seem to lead to acquittal and to an uneasily indeterminate incarceration. In this light, the death wish many critics have described as the essence of the narrator's compulsions to crime and confession would seem to be thwarted or deflected. But, if the evidence of the narrator's insanity seems clear, it is difficult to read the story with the sense that he is exonerated because of it: the recognition of his madness does not convert his condemnable "*atrocious crimes*" to pitiable "*effects of disease.*" This may be due in part to the pride and arrogance of the narrator's intellect. It is due even more to the way the elements of the madness figure in the acts themselves. . . .

The pattern of the narrator seeking to defend his rationality but revealing instead his partial insanity is replicated in "The Black Cat." In this case, the issue of a charge of insanity is more oblique and subtle. It is suggested initially by the "indeed" in his opening observation: "For the most wild, yet most homely narrative which I am about to pen, I neither expect nor solicit belief. Mad indeed would I be to expect it." The implication of this seems to be that some have thought him mad, either for his acts or, perhaps, for his babblings about a persecuting demon cat. Or, at least, by laying his account of events before the bar of reason he is inviting the charge of insanity. Like the narrator of "The Tell-Tale Heart," he is self-conscious of the imputation that something either in the nature of the events he recounts or in the manner of his relating them will signal mental imbalance. . . .

Delusion and Egotism

In "The Black Cat" this attempt at rational explanation also reveals a pattern of madness that in certain respects parallels the monomania in "The Tell-Tale Heart." In the narrator's perception of the images of a cat on the wall of the burnt house and of a gallows on the breast of Pluto's successor, both of which he interprets as signs of a demonic persecution, we may recognize elements of delusion. His increasingly obsessive fear and hatred of the cats is also, like "The Tell-Tale Heart" narrator's excess of rational planning, a motiveless distortion and perversion of what might seem an otherwise healthy human impulse, his special fondness for animals. It is important to recognize the terms of this distortion, for while the narrator's criminal behavior may be blamed on "the Fiend Intemperance," . . . the primary agents of his criminal fate were part of his nature, an excess of his distinguishing virtues: as he asserts, "From my infancy I was noted for the docility and humanity of my disposition. . . ."

Undermining the Insanity Defense

In "The Black Cat" Poe would seem again to undermine the insanity-defense argument in several ways. Paralleling the pattern in "The Tell-Tale Heart," the moral insanity of the narrator, the derangement of the affections that leads him to murder his wife out of a deflected rage against a cat, becomes in the figure of that cat the means to his exposure and punishment, the agent not of exculpation but of a kind of poetic justice. Furthermore, the arguments that locate all the terms of good and evil in the *"brute beast"* are the self-serving rationalizations of a madman. This is even more interestingly the case with the concept of "perverseness," which, like the arguments of Ray and other medical authorities, is presented as a logical, "philosophical" explanation that voids overtly immoral acts of their moral implications. . . .

At least in the . . . stories we have considered, Poe's centering of interest in "matters of psychology" can be understood not as indifference to moral issues but as a play on the treatment of those issues in the context of the insanity-defense controversy of his day. Whereas the insanity defense sought to alter radically the moral content of brutal acts, Poe's perverseness and the parallel confession compulsions in "The Tell-Tale Heart" and "The Black Cat" effect a radical restoration of their moral consequences. Both utilize a concept of obliterated will and "loss of the *use* of reason"—an aberration of normality in the insanity defense, a normality of aberration in Poe's perverseness. But, as if responding to the unsettling resolution of successful insanity defenses, the apparently incongruous disjunction between brutal acts and a response of pity or sympathy, Poe's deterministic forces lead the guilty to the hangman.

Abnormality and the Confusion of Life and Death

Charles E. May

Charles E. May is a professor emeritus of English at California State University–Long Beach and the author of several books on the short story form.

In the following excerpt May contends that Edgar Allan Poe's prose is distinctive for his time in that the narrators involve the reader in their inner lives. The tales' tight unity derives from the very obsessions at the heart of the stories. Nothing unrelated to the obsession of the main characters is allowed to enter the story. The greatest horrors are not "mass" misfortunes like wars and earthquakes, but inner catastrophes.

Nevertheless, the mental depravity of one fictional character reflects the universal condition of all humans. Insanity in Poe is often linked with confusion over the thin line between life and death, as in premature burial. Madness itself is a state of mind that mimics death.

The ultimate implication of Poe's theories of art as the highly unified and patterned creation of a bodiless ideal is the human desire to escape the consequences of being mere body by retreating into the art work itself. And indeed two of Poe's best-known stories make this simultaneously irresistible and horrible desire their central theme. . . .

Who Is Mad?

"The Fall of the House of Usher" (September 1839), [is] a story that in many ways is the complete Poe paradigm because it pulls together so many of his basic themes and embodies so

Charles E. May, *Edgar Allan Poe: A Study of the Short Fiction.* Boston: Twayne Publishers, 1991. Copyright © 1991 by G.K. Hall & Co. All rights reserved. Reproduced by permission of Gale, a part of Cengage Learning.

many of his innovative techniques. As usual, the major critical controversy concerning this story centers on the ontological nature of the events—either that Roderick is mad or the narrator is mad. . . .

One important technique Poe uses in the story is to separate his central protagonist, the embodiment of obsession and desire, from his observing self. . . . The story begins with the entrance of the narrator into the world of Usher, which is the world of the story itself. The landscape he enters . . . surrounds the house—the "rank sedges," "the white trunks of decayed trees," the "singularly dreary tract of country." . . .

The House as a Symbol of Madness

But it is the house itself that causes the narrator, and the reader, the first difficulties: "I know not how it was—but, with the first glimpse of the building, a sense of insufferable gloom pervaded my spirit." He then justifies the feeling as insufferable because it is not relieved by the poetic sentiment that usually allows one to accept the sternest natural images of the desolate and terrible. Furthermore, he says the house creates such a sense of "unredeemed dreariness of thought" that no "goading of the imagination could torture into aught of the sublime." He himself poses the hermeneutical [interpretative] questions: "what was it that so unnerved me in the contemplation of the House of Usher? It was a mystery all insoluble."

The narrator knows that some combinations of natural objects have the power of affecting one in such a way, but he also knows that the "analysis of this power lies among considerations beyond our depth." He considers that maybe a "different arrangement of the particulars of the scene, of the details of the picture, would be sufficient to modify, or perhaps to annihilate its capacity for sorrowful impression." Thus he tries the experiment of looking at the house from the perspective of its reflection in the tarn [lake], but the inverted re-

In this scene from the 1960 film House of Usher, *based on Edgar Allan Poe's short story, the residents of the house welcome the narrator.* © A.I.P./The Kobal Collection.

flected image, much like a distorted image in one of Poe's own stories, gives him a shudder more thrilling than the house itself.

It is a wonderful opening, one of the most famous in all of literature, for the narrator simulates the process by which the reader enters into the patterned reality of the art work, obviously affected, but puzzled as to what could have created such an effect. Looking into the tarn deepens what the narrator calls his superstition, for when he lifts his eyes to the house itself, he seems to perceive: "that about the whole mansion and domain there hung an atmosphere peculiar to themselves and their immediate vicinity—an atmosphere that had no affinity with the air of heaven, but which had reeked up from the decayed trees, and the gray wall, and the silent tarn—a pestilent and mystic vapor, dull, sluggish, faintly discernible, and leaden-hued." . . .

Instability of House and Mind

Although the narrator tries to shake off this dreamlike sense and observe "the real aspect of the building," he notes a further fact about its construction that points to its reality as an aesthetic object. No portion of the masonry has fallen, but "there appeared to be a wild inconsistency between its still perfect adaptation of parts, and the crumbling condition of the individual stones." The only other element of the building's "instability" is a fissure that runs from the roof to the base of the house in the tarn. Indeed, the instability of the house is like the instability of the art work itself, that gains life not because of its parts but because of its structure, but that in turn always carries within itself the means of its own deconstruction.

It is completely appropriate for this paradigmatic Poe story to feature a protagonist described in such a way that many have recognized him as Poe himself, and that the expression of his face is an arabesque one that the narrator cannot connect with any idea of "simple humanity." Indeed, Usher is not an embodiment of simple humanity, but rather is, as all Poe's protagonists are, what W.H. Auden calls a unitary state, an embodiment of desire. Like his house, there is also an "inconsistency" about Usher, an "incoherence," a sense that the parts do not fit together.

Morbid Acuteness of the Senses

Like other Poe protagonists, Usher suffers from a disease characterized by an unusual attentiveness or focus, what the narrator calls "a morbid acuteness of the senses." For Usher, this acuteness means that he finds all but the most bland food intolerable, can wear garments of only certain textures, finds the odors of flowers oppressive, cannot bear anything but the faintest light, and cannot listen to anything but some peculiar sounds from stringed instruments. It is clear that Roderick is the artist who cannot tolerate any sensory input at all; has indeed cut himself from any stimulus from the external world. . . .

Usher's fear is of no particular thing, as indeed it could not be, for he embodies that fear of ultimate nothingness faced by the protagonist in "The Pit and the Pendulum." He says he dreads events of the future, not in themselves, but in their results in terror, and feels he must soon "abandon life and reason together, in some struggle with the grim phantasm, FEAR." Usher's fear is not a plausible psychological fear, but a fear that can only be understood in aesthetic terms. His obsession centers on a family superstition about the relationship between the house and the self, in which the house affects his spirit—"an effect which the *physique* of the gray walls and turrets, and of the dim tarn into which they all looked down, had, at length, brought about upon the *morale* of his existence." And this superstitious fear is complicated by the shadowy existence of Madeline, his sister, a figure the narrator regards with the same unspeakable dread with which he regarded the house, for both house and sister represent Roderick's own inherently flawed and detested physicality.

Art and Madness

Although we know little about Roderick, we do know that he is an artist: he paints, he improvises on the guitar, and he writes poetry. His work is characterized by what the narrator calls a "highly distempered ideality" that throws a "sulphurous lustre over all." Of his paintings, the narrator says, "if ever mortal painted an idea, that mortal was Roderick Usher." Concerned only with the purest of abstraction, with no relation to objects in the world, Roderick's paintings are hermetically sealed, like the one painting the narrator describes of a rectangular vault or tunnel under the earth with no outlet and no artificial light, yet which still is bathed in intense rays.

Usher's poem, which the narrator says has an "under or mystic current" of meaning, suggests the "tottering of his lofty reason upon her throne." And indeed the poem aesthetically mirrors the story itself because it identifies the haunted palace of art with the person of Usher himself, complete with images of eyes as windows and pearl and ruby as teeth and lips at the door. The poem reflects the underlying motivation of the story that so haunts Roderick: that of the "sentience of vegetable things," an obsession that Usher pushes to the extreme theory of the "kingdom of inorganization," that is, the sentience of the structure of nonliving things, specifically the house itself.

> The conditions of the sentience had been here, he imagined, fulfilled in the method of collocation of these stones—in the order of their arrangement, as well as in that of the many *fungi* which over-spread them, and the decayed trees which stood around—above all in the long undisturbed endurance of this arrangement, and in its reduplication in the still waters of the tarn. Its evidence—the evidence of the sentience—was to be seen, he said (and I here started as he spoke), in the gradual yet certain condensation of an atmosphere of their own about the waters and the walls.

A crucial statement about the aesthetic pattern being the source of sentience, the passage reminds us that as an artist, Roderick has cut himself off from any external sensory source for his art; thus all that he has left to feed on is himself. This is a story about the ultimate romantic artist. . . .

The Universal Split and Shriek

After all this exposition and aesthetic motivation, the story moves rapidly toward its narrative portion and climax when Madeline is entombed and we discover that Roderick and Madeline are twins and that "sympathies of a scarcely intelligible nature had always existed between them." Our suspicion that Madeline's "death" is metaphorically meaningful because she is Roderick's twin is intensified when the narrator notes that her disease has left "as usual in all maladies of a strictly cataleptical character, the mockery of a faint blush upon the bosom and the face, and that suspiciously lingering smile upon the lip which is so terrible in death." The sympathy between Roderick and Madeline becomes the source of what the narrator suspects is an "oppressive secret" within Roderick that leads to an increasing tension that culminates in a storm of such whirlwind velocity that the previously mentioned atmosphere around the house enshrouds it with a luminous glow.

At this point in the story, when the narrator reads to Roderick a romance entitled the "Mad Trist," sounds described in the fiction are echoed in Roderick and the narrator's own fictional world. The shriek of the dragon in the "Mad Trist" is echoed by a shriek in "The Fall of the House of Usher," as is the terrible ringing sound of the romance hero's shield. . . .

This interface between fiction and reality brings the story to its climax as Roderick shouts, "*Madman! I tell you that she now stands without the door!*" and the utterance has the "potency of a spell"; the doors swing open and Madeline, with a moaning cry, falls inward upon Usher and, like falling cards, he falls to the floor, and the house falls into the tarn. The instability of the house, the fissure that splits it, widens, and the story deconstructs just as the house does, as everything collapses back into formulated precreation nothingness and the tale ends on the italicized words of its own title.

Madness in Poe's Tales as a Means of Escape

Daniel Hoffman

Daniel Hoffman, emeritus professor of English and former poet in residence at the University of Pennsylvania, is well known for his poetry as well as his criticism of the works of Edgar Allan Poe.

In the following excerpt Hoffman contends that Poe's tales demonstrate an effort to escape the body and intensify the spirit. The force with which his characters pursue the spirit takes them on perilous journeys into madness, sometimes through the medium of drugs and alcohol. The tales which Poe classified as arabesques are psychological studies of madmen. Identity is split, as all aspects of human character become inverted. A perverse self, hidden inside the larger self, leads the narrator to perform horrible atrocities. The total suppression of childhood and parents results in terrifying battles of conscience, impulse, and insanity.

Birthplace, parentage, ancestry—these are the attributes of body. To the soul they are inessential accidents. And the direction of Poe's mind, the thrust of his imagination is—may I restate the obvious?—away from the body and toward the spirit, away from the 'dull realities' of this world, toward the transcendent consciousness on 'a far happier star.' His protagonists are all attempting to get out of the clotted condition of their own materiality, to cross the barrier between the perceptible sensual world and that which lies beyond it. And so they undertake hazardous voyages, either into the stratosphere or to the moon; or by descending into dungeons and vaults in the earth; or down maelstroms in the sea toward the center of the very world. Others cross the bourne between our life and another by breaking through the barrier of silence and speaking from beyond the grave. Some achieve this posthumous eloquence as the result of a mesmerical [hypnotic] suspension of mortality; some, consuming inordinate amounts of laudanum [an opiate], take the trip on drugs. . . .

What characterizes the Arabesques is their exploration of extreme psychological states—the narrators or chief characters are often madmen, or persons who undergo some excruciating suffering of the soul. . . .

Seeing Double and Perversity

> Had I not been thus prolix [wordy], you might either have misunderstood me altogether, or, with the rabble, have fancied me mad. As it is, you will easily perceive that I am one of the many uncounted victims of the Imp of the Perverse.

It is evident . . . that the author is aware of deep cleavages in his own self—or, in the terminology of his time, in his soul. He appears, to himself as well as to others, as both sane and mad; as both a civil workday person who keeps appointments and earns his wages, and as a victim of the Imp of the Perverse. This Imp, it will be recalled, is that principle which compels us to 'act, for the reason that we should *not*. . . . Nor will this overwhelming tendency to do wrong for the wrong's sake, admit of analysis, or resolution into ulterior elements. It is a radical, a primitive impulse.'

Poe speaks here with unexampled knowledge of the hidden self within the self. In 'The Imp of the Perverse' he summons the courage so to expose his secret sinfulness. . . . It is his gallows confession, his confession of his confession of his motiveless crime, a crime which had been perfect except for his *double compulsion* to perform that which he should not do: first to murder his victim (no details are given as to any injury the victim may have done him), then, 'as [he] reflected upon [his] absolute security,' to confess—to rush down the street crying aloud his guilt—had otherwise been undetected. . . .

Division of the Self

Who, or what, is this Imp of the Perverse but a portion of the ego separated out from the rest, which seeks the destruction of that from which it is separated? The fact that it may seek its own destruction too does not deter it from its calamitous purpose. Life is on a collision course with death; the death-wish betrays, whenever it can, the life instinct. This seems madness, the mind undoing its own self-protective calculation by an uncontrollable, 'a radical, a primitive impulse.'

This impulse is so primitive, so uncanny, so terrifying that in 'The Imp of the Perverse' it appears only as a malignant force impelling the protagonist. . . .

Between them, 'The Imp of the Perverse' and 'The Angel of the Odd' state in outline form, as it were, many basic postulates of Poe's donnée [literary premise]: the division of the self, the destructive opposition of the death-wish and the life-wish; fear of death, blindness, suffocation (all, as Freud repeatedly shows, surrogate forms of castration-fear and fear of impotence); the unanticipated eruption of aggressive impulse, and of self-incrimination; the incurable addiction to drink (or drugs) which speeds the self-destructive impulse on its way; and the wish-fantasy of escape from all of these predicaments. . . .

Madness and Heightened Senses

There are no parents in the tales of Edgar Poe, nary a Mum nor a Dad. Instead all is symbol. And what does this total repression of both sonhood and parenthood signify but that to acknowledge such relationships is to venture into territory too dangerous, too terrifying, for specificity. Desire and hatred are alike insatiable and unallayed. But the war of superego upon the id, the endless battle between conscience and impulse, the unsleeping enmity of the self and its Imp of the Perverse—these struggles are enacted and re-enacted in Poe's work, but always in disguise.

Take 'The Tell-Tale Heart,' surely one of his nearly perfect tales. It's only four pages long, a triumph of the art of economy:

> How, then, am I mad? Hearken! and observe how health-ily—how calmly I can tell you the whole story. . . .

The events are few, the action brief. 'I' (in the story) believes himself sane because he is so calm, so methodical, so fully aware and in control of his purpose. Of course his knowledge of that purpose is limited, while his recital thereof endows the reader with a greater knowledge than his own. 'The disease,' he says right at the start, 'had sharpened my senses. . . . Above all was the sense of hearing acute. I heard all things in the heavens and in the earth. I heard many things in hell.' Now of whom can this be said but a delusional person? At the same time, mad as he is, this narrator is *the hero of sensibility*. His heightened senses bring close both heaven and hell.

His plot is motiveless. 'Object there was none. Passion there was none. I loved the old man. He had never wronged me. He had never given me insult. For his gold I had no desire.' The crime he is about to commit will be all the more terrible because apparently gratuitous. But let us not be lulled by this narrator's lack of admitted motive. He may have a motive—one which he cannot admit, even to himself.

> I think it was his eye! yes, it was this! One of his eyes resembled that of a vulture—a pale blue eye, with a film over it. Whenever it fell upon me, my blood ran cold; and so by degrees—very gradually—I made up my mind to take the life of the old man, and thus rid myself of the eye for ever.

And a paragraph later he reiterates, 'It was not the old man who vexed me, but his Evil Eye.'

Nowhere does this narrator explain what relationship, if any, exists between him and the possessor of the Evil Eye. We do, however, learn from his tale that he and the old man live under the same roof—apparently alone together, for there's no evidence of anyone else's being in the house. Is the young man the old man's servant? Odd that he would not say so. Perhaps the youth is the old man's son. Quite natural that he should not say so. 'I loved the old man. He had never wronged me. . . . I was never kinder to the old man than during the whole week before I killed him.' Such the aggressive revulsion caused by the old man's Evil Eye! . . .

Could he but rid himself of its all-seeing scrutiny, he would then be free of his subjection to time.

Killing the Disapproving Father

All the more so if the father-figure in this tale be, in one of his aspects, a Father-Figure. As, to an infant, his own natural father doubtless is. As, to the baby Eddie, his foster-father may have been. Perhaps he had even a subliminal memory of his natural father, who so early deserted him, eye and all, to the hard knocks experience held in store. So, the evil in that Evil Eye is likely a mingling of the stern reproaches of conscience with the reminder of his own subjection to time, age, and death.

To murder the possessor of such an eye would be indeed to reverse their situations. In life, the old man seems to the narrator an absolute monarch, a personage whose power over him, however benignly exercised, is nonetheless immutable. Such exactly is the degree to which a murderer dominates his victim. And so it is that the narrator does not merely do the old man in. No, he stealthily approaches the sleeping old man, in the dead of night, and ever so craftily draws nearer, then plays upon his sleeping face a single ray from his lantern. A ray like the beam of an eye. This he does each night for a week—that very week in which he was never before so kind to him during the waking hours, when the old man had his eye working.

> Upon the eighth night I was more than usually cautious in opening the door. A watch's minute hand moves more quickly than did mine. Never before that night had I *felt* the extent of my powers—of my sagacity. I could scarcely contain my feelings of triumph. To think that there I was, opening the door, little by little, and he not even to dream of my secret deeds or thoughts. . . .

The old man must have realized what was happening, what was about to happen, for

> Presently I heard a slight grown . . . not of pain or of grief— oh, no!—it was the low stifled sound that arises from the bottom of the soul when overcharged with awe. . . . I knew it well. I knew what the old man felt, and pitied him, although I chuckled at heart.

And then, breaking the darkness and the silence, he spots his ray directly 'upon the vulture eye.' 'Now, I say, there came to my ears a low, dull, quick sound, such as a watch makes when enveloped in cotton.' This is the sound, he says, of the old man's heartbeat.

Excited to a pitch of 'uncontrollable terror' by the drumbeat of his victim's heart, he gives a shout, flings wide the door of his lantern, and drags the old man to the floor. Then he suffocates him under the mattress. 'His eye would trouble me no more.'

Now, quickly, methodically, the murderer completes his work. 'First I dismembered the corpse. I cut off the head and the arms and the legs.' Then he places all between the beams under the floorboards. These he deftly replaces so that no eye could detect a thing. He had made care to catch all the blood in a tub. 'Ha! ha!' . . .

In striking the Evil Eye of the old man, the young madman strikes, symbolically, at his sexual power. Nor does this contradict the other significations I have suggested for the ocular member. As the source of conscience, of surveillance of the boy's sexual misdemeanors, and as the reminder of his subjection to his own body, the eye derives some of its powers from its linkage, in imagination, with potency. . . .

At first all is well, but as they sit, and chat, his head begins to ache, he hears a ringing in his ears. It grows in volume, '*a low, dull, quick sound . . . as a watch makes when enveloped in cotton*. . . . hark! louder! louder! *louder!*'

He could escape the Evil Eye, but not 'the beating of his hideous heart.'

Of course it was his own heart which the murderer heard beat. Would he have heard it, had not his Imp of the Perverse commanded that he lead the police to the very scene of the crime? Or was this Imp, whose impulse seems so inexplicable, his own conscience, inescapable as long as his own heart should beat, demanding punishment for the terrible crime he had wrought? Thus he is *never* free from the gaze of the old man's clear blue eye.

Confessing Shrewdness to Deny Madness in Poe's Stories

Christopher Benfey

Christopher Benfey, the Mellon Professor of English at Mount Holyoke College in Massachusetts, is the author of numerous critical reviews as well as such books as The Great Wave *and* The Double Life of Stephen Crane.

Benfey states in the following excerpt that no writer other than Sigmund Freud has received as much attention from psychoanalysts as Edgar Allan Poe. In "The Black Cat" and "The Tell-Tale Heart," the interest is not on discovering who committed the crimes but on what occurred in the minds of the madmen to cause them to murder their victims. The murderers try to convince themselves as well as the reader that being able to tell their stories coherently and provide minute details and plans proves their sanity, despite the lunacy of their actions. One sign of the madness of the narrator of "The Tell-Tale Heart" is his claim to be able to read his silent victim's mind. This operates in "The Black Cat" as well when the murderer tries to convince his audience and himself of his rationality.

Poe's critics have tended to divide into two camps: on the one hand, those who claim to have keys to the puzzles, and on the other, those who find the puzzles impossible or unworthy of solution. In the first group one finds a wealth of extraordinary psychoanalytic readings of Poe. . . .

Puzzles in the Mind

I do not propose to steer a middle course between these two camps, even if it were easy to say what such a course might be. My aim instead is to show how one kind of puzzle—

Christopher Benfey, *New Essays on Poe's Major Tales*. New York: Cambridge University Press, 1993. Copyright © Cambridge University Press 1993. Reprinted with the permission of Cambridge University Press.

perhaps not the most obvious or "crackable" kind—is at the heart of some of Poe's best known tales. This sort of puzzle concerns the ways in which people are themselves enigmas to one another: people (that is, characters) both within the stories and on either side, so to speak (the author and the reader). Poe was an early student of the ways in which human beings have access, or are denied access, to the minds of other people. . . .

Poe was fascinated by mind readers and unreadable faces, the twin fantasies of utter exposure and complete secrecy. His private eye Auguste Dupin is the preeminent example of the former. In a scene from "The Murders in the Rue Morgue," Dupin astonishes the narrator by reading his mind, having boasted that "most men, in respect to himself, wore windows in their bosoms". Dupin pulls off this feat by being extraordinarily attentive to psychological association, a process Poe relates to the solving of puzzling crimes. In "The Purloined Letter," Dupin retrieves the hidden letter by reproducing the mental calculations of the deceitful minister D. The devil, in the less familiar story "Bon-Bon," has kindred powers—he can even read the mind of a pet cat. . . .

Poe was equally interested, however, in the opposite phenomenon of the unknowable mind, the mind that remains, despite all attempts at access, ultimately mysterious. . . .

Reading Minds

It is to this theme of the unreadable in human relations that my subtitle ["Poe and the Unreadable"] refers. It is not by accident that Poe should invite us to compare reading minds with reading books, or that his stories should involve both activities. He saw the most intimate relation between these two acts of reading, constantly drawing analogies between them. We will now turn to two such tales: "The Tell-Tale Heart" and "The Black Cat." . . .

These tales are not whodunits—we know right from the start who the murderer is. They are closer to the genre now called thrillers, where the crime itself and the psychology of the killer are more the focus than the question of who committed the crime. If there is a mystery in these tales, it is the mystery of motive: not who did it but why. . . .

Poe's interest in motiveless crime, however, had less to do with human freedom than with human knowledge. He was drawn to two ideas connected with it: one, the ways in which the murderer is a mystery to himself (a dominant idea in "The Black Cat"), and two, the related ways in which the murder results from some barrier to the killer's knowledge of other people (a major theme in "The Tell-Tale Heart").

"The Tell-Tale Heart" begins *in medias res*, in the midst of things. We seem to be overhearing a conversation—one that began before our arrival on the scene—between a murderer and his interlocutor. The identity of the latter is never specified; it could be a prison warden, a doctor in a madhouse, a newspaper reporter, a judge. The very indefiniteness makes it easy for the reader to imagine that the killer is speaking directly to him or her.

> True!—nervous—very, very dreadfully nervous I had been and am; but why *will* you say that I am mad? The disease had sharpened my senses—not destroyed—not dulled them. Above all was the sense of hearing acute. I heard all things in the heaven and in the earth. I heard many things in hell. How, then, am I mad? Hearken! and observe how healthily—how calmly I can tell you the whole story.

The Diseased Mind

The first word is a concession—this speaker wants to communicate, to persuade. He thinks that by giving some ground ("granted I'm nervous"), he can win the battle ("but I'm not crazy").

In tales such as Edgar Allan Poe's "The Black Cat," the mystery is not in finding out who committed the crime but in navigating the murderer's psyche to find out the reason the crime was committed. The Library of Congress.

Like other characters in Poe's tales (and to some degree, apparently, Poe himself), the narrator believes that certain diseases of the mind can actually sharpen mental acuity. In "Eleonora," for example, another half mad speaker tries to persuade us that he is sane: "Men have called me mad," he says, "but the question is not yet settled . . . whether all that is profound—does not spring from disease of thought—from *moods* of mind exalted at the expense of the general intellect". And when the narrator of "The Murders in the Rue Morgue" tries to explain Dupin's extraordinary powers, he remarks: "What I have described in the Frenchman was merely the result of an excited, or perhaps of a diseased intelligence". If the speaker in "The Tell-Tale Heart" is willing to admit that he's the victim of a disease, madness he will not concede. Like much else in the tale, the nature of the disease remains unspecified, unless it is the general nervousness that he mentions.

He does make perfectly clear what madness is. It is the inability to communicate. His proof of his sanity will therefore be his ability to "*tell* . . . the whole story" [my emphasis]—the verb is crucial—"healthily" and "calmly." Sanity is equated in this character's mind with telling tales. He invites us to gauge how healthily and calmly he can recount the story of the murder. . . .

For all the concision with which our speaker tells his tale, eliminating almost every detail that would help us place him in time and space, he goes on at elaborate length about things that might seem peripheral to the main plot of the story. Nearly a quarter of the narrative, for example, is devoted to the seven nights in which the narrator watches the old man sleep. Why such sustained attention to such *undramatic* behavior?

According to the narrator, this patient observation is meant to provide further and conclusive proof of his sanity. . . .

And yet, for all his secrecy, our speaker claims to have access to the mind of the old man. His very privacy, his enclosedness, seem to allow him to see into the minds of other people. . . .

Fear of Secrets Discovered

It is only after this sustained scene of mind reading versus secrecy that the old man's eye opens, and the murder is accomplished. It is precisely the breach of secrecy, the penetrating-yet-veiled eye, that seems to motivate the murder.

Poe puts unmistakable emphasis on this claim to *knowledge*: "I say I *knew* it well. I *knew* what the old man felt. . . . I *knew* that he had been lying awake" [my emphasis]. It is precisely this claim to knowledge of another's mind, especially knowledge of another's feelings of pain, that has given rise to some of the most challenging philosophical reflections in our century. . . .

The Need to Confess

"The Black Cat" was first published later the same year, 1843, as "The Tell-Tale Heart." It resembles the earlier story in several obvious ways, as though Poe were digging deeper in a familiar vein. It too purports to be a killer's confession, and the murder victim is again a member of the killer's household. This killer is also eager to assure us of his sanity: "Yet, mad am I not—and very surely do I not dream." In both stories, furthermore, the police seem almost reluctant to pursue their investigations. The killers must insist on their guilt, even offer proof of it. In each case the discovery of the concealed body is the result of the killer's own obsessive need to reveal its hiding place. . . .

Poe's murderers are not so much obsessive killers as obsessive *talkers*. Afflicted with what Poe calls in "The Black Cat" "the spirit of PERVERSENESS," their perversity lies not in their need to kill but in their need to tell. Thus, "The Imp of the Perverse" ends with the murderer's sense of safety: He's safe, he tells himself, "if I be not fool enough to make open confession". This thought is his undoing. "I well, too well understood that, to *think*, in my situation, was to be lost".

The Mad Chamber of the Mind in Poe's Poetry

Benjamin F. Fisher

Benjamin F. Fisher is professor of English at the University of Mississippi. He has written on Edgar Allan Poe and on Victorian poets.

According to Fisher in the following essay, in Poe's poems, the inner journeys were not uplifting, as they were for the American Transcendentalists, but grim and negative. Closure is reached in such poems as "The Raven" when the speaker has an awakening and, simultaneously, goes mad. The ominous, exact rhymes and rhythms of Poe's verse, so often derided by his critics, actually intensify the horror. The primary pattern of the poems remains the same: they include a mentally disturbed protagonist mourning the death of a beautiful woman. The raven is a dark, uncontrollable element of the mind. In "Ulalume," the dead woman's name, suggesting moonlight, heightens the sense of the speaker's lunacy.

Poe's canon contains some of the most widely known literary works in the world. His early desire to be a poet has been gratified many times over, if from no other source than the popularity of "The Raven," one of the best-known poems in the English language, though many more reasons for such reputation exist. The early "To Helen ('Helen, thy beauty is to me . . .')," "The Sleeper," "The City in the Sea," "The Coliseum," "Sonnet—To Science," "The Bells," "Annabel Lee," "Ulalume" and "Eldorado": all are well known. Poe's critical dicta are likewise familiar and repeatedly cited, e.g. that a "long poem" is a contradiction in terms, that poetry must have a

Benjamin F. Fisher, _The Cambridge Introduction to Edgar Allan Poe_. New York: Cambridge University Press, 2008. Copyright © Benjamin F. Fisher 2008. Reprinted with the permission of Cambridge University Press.

distinctive "music," that prose inclines more toward truth than poetry (beauty is the aim of poetry), that the brief prose tale is the greatest form in fiction, that the ideal reading time spans no more than an hour and a half. . . .

Grim Results of Psychological Exploration

During [the era of American Romanticism] strong individualism was often promoted as an essential to living everyday life. The nation was still new, so its maturing process or being on the move, so to call it, brought about discoveries of confrontations with much that was relatively unknown. What may have seemed to be an unlimited number of discoveries yet to be made in moving across the land fostered an understandable desire to have what was discovered be beneficial. Investigating what was still new territory bore resemblances to exploring the human mind. In his essay "The Poet," [Ralph Waldo] Emerson stated that America itself was a great poem. Since poems do not function explicitly in wholly rational planes, the mind seemed to contain much that was subjective. Emerson and those who subscribed to his ideas thought that exploring the human mind/self would reveal overwhelmingly positive discoveries. . . .

Skeptics argued that while exploration of the mind/self was necessary and exciting, the discoveries might be grim. Journeying into the human mind/self might in fact reveal twisted and shadowy corridors instead of those brilliantly illuminated spacious areas, as characteristic of the self, the predominant concern in many important American texts, and therefore Emerson's reiterated motifs of light (usually the natural light associated with sun, moon, stars because the technology of lighting that we take for granted today did not then exist) and flowing water were refashioned into harsh, glaring illumination or overcast with vast darkness or as weird, terrifying lakes and seas. All were ambiguous, hence unsettling.

Poe's poems and fiction, which typically evince these latter qualities, are rife with decaying buildings and dreary landscapes (and seascapes), winding corridors that appear to be labyrinthine, spiral staircases (and other spiral motifs). . . .

Death in Life

Poe was intent on demonstrating that the protagonist's terrors originate in and emanate from the mind, the "soul," to use his term in the "Preface" to *Tales of the Grotesque and Arabesque*. He contended that those who perceived only "German" (i.e. facile Gothic) substance in his tales overlooked his subtle modifications of terrors to function as credible psychological states (in all but a few of the tales). Where Poe learned about the nature of the mind/self is immaterial. The uses to which he put such education are his major artistic achievement. Many of his creative writings operate as dream structures, a fitting technique in psychological literature. A work opens with what appears to be credibility on the speaker-narrator's part, then shifts into increasingly dreamlike or fantastic planes. The lyric poem and the short story are perfect frames for such mindsets, and, as a dream may end, many of Poe's works lead us to an explosive conclusion. In effect, the protagonist awakens, or perhaps dies—dying an actual death or entering death-in-life, for example madness—providing closure as well for readers. . . .

Emotionally Disturbed Speakers

Poe's output of verse is small compared with that of his fiction and critical writing, and compared with the far greater quantities of verse published by poets such as [John] Milton, [Alfred] Tennyson, [Walt] Whitman, [Emily] Dickinson, [E.A.] Robinson or [Robert] Frost, an irony because Poe wished to be recognized chiefly as a poet. Moreover, his poems, for the most part, contain such emphatic stanzaic patterns and rhymes that to some they do not seem to be serious art. Much more than mere sound (and no sense) informs Poe's poetry, as careful reading reveals. Although Ralph Waldo Emerson once spoke dismissively of Poe as the "jingle man," his remark was made after the very different verse of Walt Whitman had appeared, so the elderly Emerson may no longer have cared for the pronounced rhymes and rhythms typical in Poe's verse. Sound is crucial in Poe's poems, but sound does not subsume psychological plausibility; instead the sound promotes our apprehension of the sense, and that coalescence produces the success of the individual poem. Most of Poe's poems reveal emphatic rhyme schemes, but he could also achieve effective art in blank verse, especially in "The Coliseum"—although subtle rhymings enhance that poem.

Another fact worth remembering: Poe is not the protagonist in most of his poems (or in his tales). Instead his imaginative writings reveal very little influence from his personal circumstances, despite what much long-lasting mythology would suggest to the contrary. . . .

Poe's poetry and fiction may convey considerable subjectivity, but that subjectivity emanates from the speaker within the poem rather than serving as a barometer to Poe's personal feelings. . . .

Poe's poems display repeated themes and situations. First, his protagonist-speakers are males, who are usually emotionally disturbed, chiefly from the loss of a beloved woman. At times the protagonists are journeying, not so much over actual physical geographical terrain as in geography of the imagination, symbolized by means of landscape or other tangible details in setting. The speaker's overwrought mind makes him (they are all male) unreliable about his own state and correspondingly about what he perceives as he attempts to convey actualities in his circumstances. . . .

Since the Romantic impulse in Great Britain tended to poetic expression, whether in verse or prose, Poe naturally gravitated toward such forms. Much Romantic writing centered in landscape because of a renewed awareness of and interest in Nature, especially in its untamed state. Often, natural phenomena symbolized states in the human mind. A second important feature in Romantic writing was that of the introspective character, who appeared repeatedly in contemporaneous literature. Staunchly individualistic, despite circumstances that strongly militated against the wisdom of maintaining such a stance, the Romantic loner-hero became a major presence in the literature of the era. . . .

Moving Toward Irrationality

Not for nothing do several of Poe's poems bear titles with the word "dream" being the operative term, and the majority of his poems may be reasonably likened to dream structures. A Poe poem begins, typically, in some mundane situation, then moves the speaker and readers into less rational planes. There we behold visionary scenes which, combined with the insistent, if monotonous, "music," draw us, just as dreaming does, away from everyday life into a fantastic world, a geography of the imagination rather than a mundane landscape. . . .

Delusions in "The Raven"

"The Raven" has often been construed as a wholly supernatural poem, which, because of folklore that links ravens to the devil, offers one convincing approach to the poem. Equally convincing are the conditions that give credence to a non-supernatural interpretation, in which the speaker's delusions prompt him subjectively to incline *toward* supernatural underpinnings for his interaction with the raven. Poe plays upon the age-old gambit of a supernatural animal taking control of human victims, handling that theme in convincing fashion. The speaker's reading in those books of "forgotten lore," i.e. books of magic, may, in combination with the chanting effect in the rhythm of the poem, be all that is required to invoke an otherworldly presence, which takes the form of a raven.

The bird is from a world outside the speaker's chamber (a chamber that may symbolize his mind/self), and, as is so typical in literary works in which supernaturalism operates forcibly, the non-rational world represented by the bird is not subject to human control. That the speaker has attempted to mitigate his grief by reading books of magic, which may contain spells appropriate for summoning supernatural creatures, is understandable. . . .

Animal force triumphs over human reason, leaving the speaker motionless and speechless, as the repeated "still" makes clear.

Another convincing approach is that the speaker is utterly beset by grief, and that, as is suggested in many other creative works of Poe's, his is the loss of an ideal, symbolized in Lenore, who may have been no actual physical woman, but an emotional force that has nurtured the speaker's own emotional well-being. How he has managed to lose that part of what should be his fully integrated self is unclear, but in its absence he yields to notions of otherworldly influences, indicated, first, by his turning to books on magic and, second, by his attributing supernatural qualities to the raven, which in actuality it does not possess. Such a reading places "The Raven" as a solid psychological poem, in which the speaker manages to betray his own mental instability as the cause of terrors that lead to his ultimate loss of volition. This speaker appears to be only too ready to perceive his surroundings, which represent his own mindset, as those of Gothic horror. The midnight hour, his loneliness, the odd books he has been perusing until he becomes drowsy, the "ghost" on the floor, his bewilderment concerning origins of the rapping sound, his reluctance to open the door and window to his chamber (that is, to look outside himself?), and his reactions to the raven once he admits the bird: all hint of mystery and foreboding. . . .

"Ulalume" and Lunacy

In "Ulalume," wandering with his companion, Psyche (representative of his own nurturing emotions), the speaker unheedingly draws near the tomb of Ulalume, whose death has rendered him irrational. As in "The Sleeper," where moon madness (lunacy) initially overwhelms the speaker, we encounter in "Ulalume" astrological lore concerning planetary causes for troubled love. The name of Ulalume, suggestive of moonlight, may also point to lunacy in the speaker. Events in the poem may plausibly occur on Hallowe'en, when temporary influence of supernatural powers may motivate the speaker's forlorn quest. As if he anticipated present-day customs of trick or treating, Poe so situates the speaker and Psyche that the eerie circumstances of the October night make the speaker ignore Psyche's cautioning him to turn from death-related circumstances. That their journey concludes at Ulalume's tomb brings death-in-life (what a perverse treat) to him; like many other Romantic characters, the speaker cannot cope with reality.

Death, Sex, and Horror in Poe's Poetry

Edward H. Davidson

Edward H. Davidson, a critic in early American studies and literature, taught English at the University of Illinois–Urbana–Champaign.

In the following excerpt Davidson studies the connections between death, sex, the view of women, and horror, in the cultural context of Edgar Allan Poe's day. The woman of Poe's poems is overwhelmed by the man, thus losing her identity, or "dying," at the time she marries him. Sexuality itself is equivalent to dying, and dying is fraught with sensuality. This is taken to the extreme of sickness in the minds of the narrators. Poe's horror is a state in which reason and choice have been "suspended." The mad protagonists are destroyed by their own egos, which keep them from learning anything. The speaker in "The Raven" is typical of the poetic protagonist who finds the coherence of the world and of his own mind shattered in a moment of horror. From this shattered ego, however, may come a vision of ultimate truth.

If death were specially dignified in the middle-class culture of the early nineteenth century and reached in Poe one of its most significant, and contemporary, expressions, so too was death then as always very close to sexual love. The metaphysical [poet]s in the age of [English poet John] Donne were not the first to discover that one could love into death and die into love or that, in each act of love's consummation, one came closer to death. In a later economic property structure

Edward H. Davidson, *Poe: A Critical Study*. Cambridge, MA: The Belknap Press of Harvard University Press, 1957. Copyright © 1957 by the President and Fellows of Harvard College. All rights reserved. Copyright renewed 1985 by Edward H. Davidson. Reproduced by permission of Harvard University Press.

one may well "die into love" at the very moment of union: at marriage the woman "dies" by changing her name and identity for the sake of receiving her husband's name and identity; therefore, in the nature of a "union the two" comes a denial of the separateness of the one. . . .

Connection of Love and Death

Woman in death became equated with woman at marriage: the corpse was the bride, and the grave clothes were the bridal dress. Woman as a sacrificial emblem in the allurements and pieties of marriage reached the ultimate sacrifice in dying. (In an age when many women did die young after their many miscarriages and child-bearing, death indeed became a kind of second dying to which marriage had been the first.) The wedding and the burial service became a nearly duplicate ritual: the wedding gown was the shroud; the hand, tremulous and cold at the wedding ceremony, was the hand cold in death; and the burial office reënacted the wedding ceremony. (As in love and life, the woman could be appealed to and wooed all over again in death.) (Poe's poems and tales are ritual incantations to the erotically desirable young woman who is forever white, aloof, reserved, virginal, bridal, whether she lies on the wedding bed or the funeral bier.) This commingling of the living and the dead woman as infinitely desirable is nowhere better suggested than in a passage in "Morella": "And in the contour of the high forehead, and in the ringlets of the silken hair, and in the wan fingers which buried themselves therein, and in the sad musical tones of her speech, and above all . . . in the phrases and expressions of the dead on the lips of the loved and the living, I found food for consuming thought and horror. . . ."

Hidden Sexuality in Death

Behind these popular designs of woman in death was gathered the force of a reading public which had only recently been released into a world of imagination and was demanding that these themes and tantalizing rituals, hitherto consigned to bawdry and the word-of-mouth story, be expressed in both popular and moral appeals. We say, now long afterward, that death was "sentimentalized"; what we mean is that the terror of death was concealed behind a set of masks and mimes which were part of that substitute reality any reading public enjoys. Poe was the cleverest man of his time in setting up these disguises for horror and not the horror itself. Death became not an event or an action nor a condition of total nonbeing but a series of seductive postures. Children may not have died, nor did men, but women did, by the thousands in the popular poetry and song of the era; and in the beautiful young woman, the flush of life still on her cheek, her eyes just closed in her last sleep, the chamber arrayed for her final rites, the age found its satisfactory counterpart for the overripe, bosomy, hoydenish [boisterous] or simpering, creatures who had been similarly gratifying creatures of substitute passion in an age just past—or in one soon to come.

If Poe succeeded in giving form to other amorphous shapes of death in the popular American mind, he more than succeeded in becoming the laureate of death and love as part of democratic individualism and the economic success story. What gave the American belief of life after death its special poignancy was the generally held faith that there could be no true *physical* death. . . .

Ruin in Past and Present

In America . . . the romantic version of ruin and decay met head-on the parvenu industrialism and its offspring, the doctrine of progress. . . .

What prophet and poet saw alike was the modern world of ruin, a world which raised up and then ruthlessly demolished its structures within a year or at most a lifetime. The change from virgin timber to smoke-blackened walls was everywhere apparent from Birmingham, England, to the Connecticut Valley and Lowell, Massachusetts. Ruin became almost an obsession; for it was a dual philosophy of ruin—that of antiquity, glorious and colorful and deeply limned with meanings for the present, and that of the contemporary world, with its inglorious grime and the disgraced landscapes. . . .

Reason Suspended in Horror

Death and horror would seem to be associated, and indeed they must be in any investigation of the mind and art of Poe. But we must now consider the theme of horror as something apart and as available for inquiry for its own sake. We must also consider this theme, as we have the topic of death, as contained in both the poetry and the short stories, though our emphasis will of necessity fall on the poetry. Yet it was such a theme as that of death or horror which binds Poe's story-writing career to his poetic experience and writing; by only slightly shifting the emphasis and the rhetorical devices he could write "tales of horror" just as ably as he had written poems of horror, and then come back, in his later life, to write poems of death and horror again. One might easily draw a line from the very early "Tamerlane" through "The Fall of the House of Usher" to "The Raven": all of them were studies of stages in consciousness when the real world slipped away or disintegrated and the mind found itself fronting the "horror" of its own loneliness and loss.

First of all, we might define the Poesque version of horror as that region or mysterious middle ground where the normal, rational faculties of thinking and choice have, for reasons beyond knowing, been suspended; ethical and religious beliefs are still the portion of men, but are powerless to function. All power of choice and all sense of direction have been lost; in fact, they have been so long lost that the nightmare world of presumed reality obeys no laws of reason or stability. It is a highly complex metaphysical condition wherein the constants of heaven and hell are fixed at their opposite polarity, but between them is the vast region wherein the human will is situated and is powerless to effect any variation of its own existence. . . .

Horror is, then, the urgent need for moral knowledge and direction—and its total lack. . . .

A Nightmare World

With Poe we are hardly concerned with "evil" at all, insofar as evil might be considered inherent in man or in the phenomenal order; in a sense, his one prescription for evil is its absence: never to know evil nor to have been engaged in any moral struggle is the condition of horror in which the Poe protagonist must exist. In such a nightmare world all the prescriptions for evil and good are matters for nostalgia and regret; they were part of some other state of being from which man has moved or which has long passed from the earth. . . .

Symbols for Psychological States

Horror was, however, not only a philosophy or a method of explaining the mystery of the universe; it was also "psychology" or a method of inquiring into special states of mind. It was a means to externalize, in vivid physical objects, inner states of being and a method of portraying the mind's awareness of itself. These "objects" of horror were not themselves necessarily horrible; they were what they were because a mind saw them and was even destroyed by them. In one way this was Poe's contribution to the dark subliminal literature of a later time: he demonstrated that states of consciousness are not simply isolated conditions of madness but are somehow intimately and intricately related to the physical world around it. Poe's fault . . . was that, once he had found a vivid externalization for a condition of inner consciousness—a crack in the wall, a black cat, a portrait, an insistent heartbeat—the physical exemplification assumed command; and in the succeeding narrative, whether in poem or in short story, the objectification was out of all proportion to the inner condition. . . .

The Overwhelming Ego

One obvious quality of the protagonist or "I" in these discourses was its inhuman arrogance and self-exaltation. This was the frame within which the Romantic ego functioned: it had to expunge its weaker, grosser self, to descend into a private hell, to suffer self-loss, and to rise again. . . .

What marks Poe's studies of a man caught in some inner or outer horror is that, for all the sufferings the protagonist must undergo, the fictive "I" never learns anything. The anguish is wasted because the sufferer comes out of the action precisely the same as he went into it. Nothing has really occurred "inside"; there was no inner consciousness to begin with. . . .

The Maddening Insight

These tales were Poe's rationalizations of horror; that is, the principle of horror itself seems to imply that the horrific is that which suddenly interrupts or shatters the rational order of the universe; however completely that order is restored, the human mind forced to endure that "apocalypse" or shock will be forever dislocated or maddened. The young man in "The Raven" will never recover his "soul" or his acceptance of the coherence of things after his terrible insight, not only into his own madness, but into the madness of the universe itself. The young man in "The Pit and the Pendulum" was able to maintain his sanity by the power of his will to escape the swinging knife-blade just long enough to be fortuitously rescued from a private psychic world which every moment threatened him with insanity and annihilation. These and other inquiries into the dark world of the mind suggest that Poe, however much his horror was a rather simple externalization of inner states of being, was demonstrating that horror itself or various phases of loss of self might be ways into farther and deeper understanding. Horror, madness, and death are man's avenues into the ultimate rationale of existence of which our own mortal existence is but a crude fragment. Man in his earthly habit lives on the virtually unquestioned assumption that he can predict and understand nearly every event that occurs in his own life and in the diurnal motions of the planets; Poe, however much his rhetoric may have been apocalyptic and frenzied and his narrative struggling to be *outré* [a violation of convention], was nevertheless writing a series of quite moral poems and tales concerning the evidence everywhere before man's eyes of the total disunity and incoherence of his own life which is an infinitesimal part of the universal "plot of God." Man must, however, be terrified or driven to comprehend that what seems to be fractured is actually a segment of the universal design and what appears to be madness may be "divinest sense."

Insanity as the Way to Salvation in "The Pit and the Pendulum"

James Lundquist

James Lundquist is a prolific writer who has published books on Chester Himes, J.D. Salinger, Sinclair Lewis, Kurt Vonnegut, and others.

Lundquist argues in the following selection that a fragmentation of the faculties and overdevelopment of one faculty (which he calls hypertrophy) leads to an abnormal mental state in the protagonists of Poe's poems and stories. As one faculty becomes enfeebled or overintensified, the character loses all balance. Lundquist is convinced that the protagonist of "The Pit and the Pendulum" differs from Poe's other characters in that the protagonist's three main faculties are integrated at first and he can use them to struggle against his abominable situation to find the truth. The problem is that the truth is horrifying, and a sane realization of it is more terrifying than madness. Each of his defenses, including rationality, abandons him one at a time until, in his despair, he screams and gives up all hope. Only then does a hand reach out to rescue him.

The horror that runs through many [of Poe's] stories and poems ... depends directly upon the hypertrophy [overdevelopment] of a faculty. It is not merely the death embrace at the end of "The Fall of the House of Usher" that evokes terror, but also the realization that Roderick has *heard* the first faint struggles of Madeline in her coffin and lacked the *will* to release her.

James Lundquist, "The Moral of Averted Descent: The Failure of Sanity in 'The Pit and the Pendulum,'" *Poe Newsletter*, vol. II, April 1969, pp. 25–26. Reproduced by permission of the publisher and author.

Sanity and Terror

In "The Pit and the Pendulum" we have a more complicated kind of horror and perhaps a different kind of horror story. The hero again and again escapes from a terrifying situation only to find himself in worse trouble; but, curiously, the hero is integrated rather than disintegrated—one of the few Poe characters to struggle against his condition with all three faculties [feeling, intellect, and will] functioning together. He is among the *sanest* of Poe's characters, but his dilemma is the most terrifying, for when he attains psychic harmony under extreme physical and mental duress he finds that his unified powers of knowledge, feeling, and will reveal, to his great horror, his own hopelessness. Because of the limitations imposed upon him by an inquisitionary force, every act of balance or sanity only leads to a worsening of his situation; this paradox suggests that while Poe ordinarily remained true to his conception of the torture of the disordered personality, he did not overlook the possibility that sanity can be more terrifying than madness.

Three crises of sanity confront Poe's narrator in "The Pit and the Pendulum," each initially based on a primitive form of feeling or sensation from which a more complex form of feeling (emotional terror) arises. The first crisis occurs after the prisoner awakens in the darkened cell. Because he cannot see, the hero is handicapped in his effort to *comprehend* his condition; but his *will* to explore is strong enough to make up for his blindness, and with great ingenuity in manipulating his remaining senses, and with some luck, he discovers the pit. Averting what would have been a fairly sudden death only increases the horror of his situation, however, for after falling asleep in a corner he revives to find that he is strapped down beneath the swinging pendulum. This is the second crisis, and under the impetus of strong emotion (*feeling*) he pulls himself together in an attempt to escape. His strong *will* drives him to *think* of a solution, which becomes apparent the moment he recalls the salty taste (*sensation*) of the food in the dish beside him. Feeling, intellect, and will function together, and the hero escapes the pendulum—but he escapes into a more restricted and horrible situation. "I had but escaped death in one form of agony, to be delivered unto worse than death in some other," he says, as he enters the third and most horrible crisis. Even though the three faculties are perfectly unified when the glowing walls begin to close in, sanity can no longer help the hero. Through his feeling, his intellect, and his will, he comprehends his predicament and wants to escape, but there is no alternative left. He is completely limited this time, for no adjustment of the faculties can help him. His previous escapes have worsened his condition to the point where he gives up hope and yields at last to an overwhelming hypertrophy of feeling: "the agony of my soul found vent in one loud, long, and final scream of despair".

The Faculties Fighting Together

In "The Pit and the Pendulum," then, we have the hero paradoxically overcoming his limitations through the integration of his faculties only to find himself more and more limited, and finally reduced to mere feeling. In the darkened cell he is limited by the deprivation of sight; this hampers his ability to *know*. But his *will* compensates for this deficiency and he *feels* his way around the cell until he discovers the pit. Strapped on the wooden framework the hero is limited in his ability to *act*; but his *intellect* and *senses* work together to make action possible. With the glowing walls forcing him toward the pit, however, he is finally limited in his very ability to *choose*; and feeling, intellect, and will, even if unified, are no help. Each effort by the hero leads to a worse horror; the more adept he becomes at solving problems through the unification of his faculties, the more difficult the problems become, until at last they are beyond his ability to cope with them....

Salvation Through Insanity

But the crucial point in the story is not in the gradation of horror; it is in the incredible resolution. As supreme as the hero's efforts are, they only serve to delay his destruction. Ultimate salvation must come from outside himself—and in this, it would seem, lies the moral statement of "The Pit and the Pendulum." The anonymous hero condemned for an unknown, or at least unstated, crime by a merciless Inquisition apparently represents mankind condemned by a vindictive power for an almost forgotten sin. His sentence is not immediate death but life lived amid horror, which he is limited in his ability to comprehend and from which he can never escape through his own exertion. In the context of a parable of man, the moral purpose of his sentence is seemingly to diminish his faith in his own power. But the moment he gives up and commits himself to the final descent into the pit, the moment he gives up any hope of saving himself, an arm reaches out and saves him. This unexpected salvation gives the story a pattern of moral allegory that would at first seem to contradict Poe's own critical objections to didacticism [using a story to educate or inform]. . . .

In "The Pit and the Pendulum" the form and action of religious experience centers around the paradox of sanity. Poe's hero endures the multi-leveled horror that arises out of the limitations imposed upon the fully functioning man who first finds himself limited in his ability to know, then in his ability to act, and finally in his ability to choose. But his perseverance . . . , while it solves one problem always leads to another, and the integrated personality survives to endure horrors that the disintegrated personality would never have had to face. It is precisely the hero's ability to survive, however, that leads to his redemption; had he not been able to hold out until the moment of grace, for him, as it is for many of Poe's other protagonists, there would have been no Lasalle. The moral is similar to that wry explanation [poet Robert] Browning gave

of "Childe Roland to the Dark Tower Came": "He that en-
dureth to the end shall be saved." Or, to put it another way, to
enter heaven a man must first go through hell. What Poe
achieves in the abrupt narrative twist of "The Pit and the Pendulum" is a perverse vision of hope amid despair; and this,
more than the disintegration of personality may be the great
subject that he discovered.

Poe's Fixation on the Death of Beautiful Women

Karen Weekes

Karen Weekes, a professor of English and women's studies, heads the Division of Arts and Humanities at Pennsylvania State University at Abington.

In the following excerpt Weekes posits that Edgar Allan Poe's tales and poetry reflect his philosophy that the most poetic subject on earth is the death of a beautiful woman. This becomes the chief obsession of Poe's narrators and, some would argue, of Poe himself. Usually, the female subjects are never developed characters in their own right. They are merely "props for the purposes of the narrator's emotional excesses." There is always an element of madness in the male character's response. Often that madness is inflamed by alcohol or opium. The sick and obsessive relationships with women always entail the woman's physical appearance, especially her eyes, her sickliness, and her death. The passivity and degeneration of some of Poe's women intensify the hero's imbalance. In the case of Ligeia and Morella, however, it is the power of the woman's will that causes the men's total collapse.

Poe's vision of the feminine ideal appears throughout his work, in his poetry and short stories, and his critical essays, most notably "The Philosophy of Composition." Especially in his poetry, he idealizes the vulnerability of woman, a portrayal that extends into his fiction in stories such as "Eleonora" and "The Fall of the House of Usher." In these tales, and even more so in "Morella" and "Ligeia," the heroines' unexpected capacities for life beyond the grave indicate that fe-

Karen Weekes, *The Cambridge Companion to Edgar Allan Poe*. New York: Cambridge University Press, 2002. Copyright © Cambridge University Press 2002. Reprinted with the permission of Cambridge University Press.

males may have more strength and initiative than the delicate models of his verse. The most significant trait of his ideal, however, is her role as emotional catalyst for her partner. The romanticized woman is much more significant in her impact on Poe's narrators than in her own right. . . .

Women as Objects

Poe's female characters thus become a receptacle for their narrator's angst and guilt, a *tabula rasa* [blank slate], on which the lover inscribes his own needs. His fictional "ideal" is a woman who can be subsumed into another's ego and who has no need to tell her own tale; she is killed off so quickly that her silence is inscribed quite irrevocably. . . . I join other critics in arguing that Poe never truly wrote about women at all, writing instead about a female object and ignoring dimensions of character that add depth or believability to these repeated stereotypes of the beautiful damsel. . . . It is hard to determine which repeated treatment of women is more demeaning: to see them as creatures in their own right, but ones who must die in order to serve a larger, androcentric [male-centered] purpose, or to utilize them as lifeless pasteboard props for the purposes of the narrator's emotional excesses.

Poe's feminine ideal thus is merely a placeholder, the less obtrusive the better, for some need in the narrator himself. As Joan Dayan remarks, Poe's tales about women "are about the men who narrate the unspeakable remembrance." Just as Poe's female characters have similarities in demeanor, his narrators peculiarly resemble each other as well. These bereaved men wax eloquent on the subject of the beauty of their spouses, but even in the cataloguing of features, Poe uses "attributes repeated and recycled no matter for whom or when he wrote, [and] the writer himself seems to be most 'heartfelt' when most vague. Poe's narrators . . . become as vain, abstract, and diseased as their objects of desire." This vagueness is evident when they attempt to describe the nature of the disease that fells these women. When Berenice is stricken, the narrator reports that "a fatal disease—fell like the simoom [a desert wind] upon her frame, and, even while I gazed upon her, the spirit of change swept over her, pervading her mind, her habits, and her character, and, in a manner the most subtle and terrible, disturbing even the identity of her person!" *How* she is changed is never delineated; we are only persuaded that the narrator believes it is for the worse.

Woman's Illness Terrifies

These males also have surprising lapses about quite significant points; Ligeia's husband not only does not remember her last name, he asserts that he may never have known it, a quite surprising admission from someone whose vast wealth derives from inheriting her presumably paternal riches. They marry for unknown reasons at questionable times: Berenice is betrothed only after she is fatally ill, and Morella and her husband are bound by "fate" despite the narrator's lack of love or passion for her. The narrators are obviously repelled by visible signs of their partner's illness ("Berenice," "Morella") and seem curiously removed from physical passion or any vestige of empathy for their wives. When they are overcome with emotion, they become corpse-like: as the narrator reads the words of Ebn Zaiat in "Berenice," the blood congeals in his veins. Upon the revivification of Rowena, the narrator's heart ceases beating and his limbs grow rigid; the ultimate sight of Ligeia's face renders him cold as stone. The vision of Madeline Usher sends that story's narrator into a stupor.

[Critic] Mary Oliver conflates these figures into "a single sensibility, as one character," and sees this persona as "other than rational. He is a man of nervous temperament; he is capable of great love, loyalty, grief, of 'wild excitement' (a recurring phrase); he owns a strange and unfettered imagination. . . . The question of madness is always present. The actions of the

An illustration of Edgar Allan Poe's "Ligeia." Karen Weekes argues that Poe's idealized woman is vulnerable and passive and that powerful women like Ligeia are depicted as horrifying. © Llebrecht Music and Arts Photo Library/ Alamy.

narrator are often clearly, recognizably insane. . . . Illness, as well, is a presence, an excuse." Opium use is another rationale for the narrator's incredible behavior. Oliver's designation of these characters as mad would certainly be a logical conclusion based on their actions as well as their "wild words." Their odd betrothals or marriages (to cousins, in two cases) are the least of their strange indulgences, as one later violates his fiancée's grave to extract her teeth and take them to his library, one builds a bedroom filled with sarcophagi and literally frightens his bride to death, one does not name his daughter until she is ten years old (and then gives her the name of the deceased mother whom he abhorred and of whom he has never spoken to the child), and one helps his emotionally deranged friend entomb a living woman. . . .

Reviled and Idealized

Once a woman steps out of the narrow boundaries of the stereotypical feminine role, she is reviled rather than revered. This argument is borne out by others of Poe's tales, including Eleonora, Berenice, and Morella.

Eleonora epitomizes Poe's ideal: young, unlearned, impressionable, and completely dedicated to her love for him. Only fifteen years old, compared with her lover's age of twenty, she is, significantly, also his cousin. A combination of the poetic ideal and the more complex prose females, she has eyes that are brighter than a flowing river, and, in the original publication, "the lilies of the valley were not more fair," but she also has the prerequisite "majestic forehead" and "large luminous eyes of her kindred." She is exceptionally frail and beautifully sickly, "slender even to fragility," with an "exceeding delicacy" of frame. Her complexion speaks "painfully of the feeble tenure by which she held existence." After plumbing the depths of "the fervor of her love" for the narrator, her main concern at death is whether the narrator will remain true to her memory or will marry another. These scenes are reminiscent of Ligeia's "idolatrous love" and the narrator's subsequent remarriage in that tale. . . .

Eleonora's love is as all-consuming as the narrator could wish, but her jealous acceptance of the promise of fidelity introduces a question of power that does not arise in the poetry, in which Poe's females are romantically submissive. However, the power struggle is absolutely resolved in favor of the narrator, who not only loves Ermengarde with the passion he once felt for Eleonora, he even denigrates the previous relationship, thus proving faithless not only to his pledge but also to the memory of his earlier beloved. Conveniently, the "Spirit of Love" absolves the narrator for breaking his vow, removes whatever curse has been invoked by his marrying Ermengarde, and releases him from the claims of Eleonora. First published in 1841, this tale is perhaps wishful thinking on Poe's part as [his wife's] Virginia's illness intensifies. However, earlier tales of conflicted emotion emphasize the narrator's struggle with strong-willed, threatening women. . . .

The silent Berenice at first seems remarkably similar to Eleonora: she, also, is the cousin of her betrothed, has a high, pale forehead, is "unparalleled" in her beauty, and "had loved [the narrator] long". But instead of reciprocating this love, the narrator plainly states his objectification of Berenice: "I had seen her—not as the living and breathing Berenice, but as the Berenice of a dream . . . not as a thing to admire, but to analyze—not as an object of love, but as the theme of the most abstruse although desultory speculation". [Critic] Jacqueline Doyle points out that as Berenice's disease progresses, this "distancing" of Egaeus from his fiancée becomes even more pronounced through his use of the definite article to describe "the" forehead, etc., rather than "her." Egaeus proposes marriage despite his passions that were purely "of the mind" and despite his revulsion at the changes wrought in her "identity"—however that is to be interpreted—by this disease.

His horror becomes unbearable as her physical condition deteriorates. When he last sees Berenice, she is drastically emaciated, and her alteration is manifested in the change in hair color from black to a "vivid yellow" that is out of keeping with her fatal state. Her sickness manifests the poetic traits to an extreme, moving from the realm of the beautiful to that of the bizarre and repellent. Her hair is an incongruous yellow, she is emaciated rather than merely slender, and her delicate pallor becomes a deathlike pall. Instead of the bright eyes of Poe's poetic heroines, hers are "lifeless, and lustreless, and seemingly pupil-less," with a "glassy stare". . . .

Upon seeing Berenice, her fiancé has already become corpse-like: he suffers an "icy chill" throughout his frame, he falls "for some time breathless and motionless." Upon seeing her teeth and ghastly smile, he wishes for death and then fades from the reader's sight into the void of the major ellipsis. The teeth are horrific because, as [critic] Liliane Weissberg points out, the "symmetry and lifeless lustre of her teeth— indicators of health and beauty—become noticeable only in their difference from the decaying body." Her emaciated, bleached features are already skeleton-like, and these teeth are a source of horror in the skull-like face.

Eroticism and Death

The narrator's terror is evoked by the specter of his own decay and demise, but an erotic specter rises before him as well. Showing one's teeth in a smile can indicate sexual interest, and if the "peculiar meaning" of Berenice's grin is of carnal desire, the cerebral narrator would be doubly overcome. The nature of Berenice's ailment has not been revealed, nor has its complete manifestation. But it has somehow altered her identity, both in her "*moral* and physical being"; Egaeus notes the "alteration produced by her unhappy malady in the *moral* condition of Berenice". If her most disturbing change is in the moral realm, one could assume that she is exchanging her innocence for sexuality, a prospect that would terrify her reclusive, passionless fiancé. Another moral shift might be her foregoing her contented, naive feminine role for that of the male sphere of knowledge, signaled by her appearing to Egaeus in his hallowed library—the site of male birth and female death.

Either interpretation involves a threat to his power in his bookish realm or in their relationship.

Whichever of these readings—Berenice as sign of mortality, as sexualized creature, or emerging New Woman—is most convincing, they are all fulfilled in Egaeus's pulling her teeth in order to gain mastery over the ideas they represent. He destroys the vision of the ghastly grinning skull and also desexualizes the corpse by removing this token of devouring carnality. The threat of the first of Poe's "Dark Ladies" has been contained, but Morella and Ligeia prove more difficult to control.

Strong Women as Objects of Horror

Ligeia and Morella both challenge the narrator in ways that Poe's stereotypical feminine heroines do not. For the narrator, the true horror in these particular "tales of terror" is that a beautiful woman can wield her own power....

The narrator is terrified by Ligeia's reappearance not so much because it means she has conquered death but because she does it through an act of vehement will, a powerful volition that renders him prostrate....

Poe's idealized woman, whose figure reappears throughout his work, is not the sexualized, intellectually overpowering Ligeia, but rather a passive, blonde version of the women who nurtured him and then died. Oliver has pointed out the similarities between the appearance of Poe's heroines and the portraits or descriptions of [his mother,] Eliza Poe, [his foster mother,] Frances Allan, and [his wife,] Virginia Clemm. Eliza and Virginia both feature a high forehead, and they all had long, black hair and dramatically dark eyes; these are features that figure prominently in Poe's descriptions. The wide or high brow and "bright" or "luminous" eyes are included in nearly every depiction of females.

Ligeia has her own voice; she writes poetry, and by having her husband recite it even places her words in his mouth.

Much more often, the narrator chooses women who are nearly speechless, as even this husband does in the person of Rowena. The poetic women are already in the grave, and the fictional ones are not far from this permanently silenced state. Stereotypical "feminine" quiescence most typifies the still-living heroine, whether she is light- or dark-featured. Even Morella and Ligeia have low, musical voices, and many have unnaturally light footsteps (Eleonora, Ligeia, Berenice).

Rather than his ideal as a partner, Ligeia is Poe's ideal of himself. She is Poe's own version of Madeline Usher: his haunting, beautiful twin. Berenice, Morella, and Madeline Usher, the other "Dark Ladies," are not eulogized to nearly the same extent as the fair, ethereal beings in the poetry. Even Ligeia's husband travels only a few months before buying a home and preparing it for his new bride, while Eleonora's husband languishes for years before courting Ermengarde. Gentle, vulnerable, delicate females, such as Eleonora and Annabel Lee, pose no sexual or intellectual threat, and their sudden, poignant deaths serve several purposes: they end the relationship while it is still in its early stages of absolute devotion, and they prevent the narrator from having to face the grisly terms of his own mortality. But most importantly for Poe, their dying serves the poetic purpose of enhancing the male's experience of melancholy Beauty, "that pleasure . . . at once the most intense, the most elevating, and the most pure".

"Ligeia" as a Tale of Obsession and Hallucination

Roy P. Basler

Roy P. Basler taught literature at the University of Arkansas. His Sex, Symbolism, and Psychology in Literature *has long been regarded as a seminal work in Freudian interpretation of such writers as Samuel Taylor Coleridge, Alfred Lord Tennyson, and Edgar Allan Poe.*

Basler was one of the first critics to discard the usual supernatural readings of Edgar Allan Poe for psychological ones. He argues in the following selection that obsession in "Ligeia," "Morella," and "Berenice" illustrates the personal ruin brought on by a fixed idea—monomania. The narrators are driven by three concepts: the power of the spirit or psyche over the physical, frustrated love and eroticism, and sensual disappointment. The narrator of "Ligeia" is fixated on the idea that he can achieve a kind of godhood through his beloved. She is his way to power, knowledge, and immortality. After Ligeia's death, he perversely and single-mindedly decides to will her back to life by providing the body—his wife Rowena—for Ligeia to inhabit. He is an ironic narrator, conveying to his listeners more that he understands himself, declaring that Ligeia is resurrected, whereas he is hallucinating after having murdered Rowena himself.

Although a number of biographers, psychoanalytical and otherwise, have employed the data and theories of several schools of thought in nonrational psychology in attempting to interpret the personality of Poe, and have indicated the need for such an approach in the interpretation of much of his writing, no one, as far as I am aware, has undertaken to point out the specific bearing of nonrational psychology on the critical interpretation of a number of Poe's stories which in their entire context seem to indicate that Poe dealt deliberately with the psychological themes of obsession and madness. Such a story is "Ligeia," the most important of a group of stories ... which includes the kindred pieces "Morella" and "Berenice."

Three Themes of Obsession

Each of these three tales shows a similar pre-occupation with the *idée fixe* [fixed idea] or obsession in an extreme form of monomania which seems intended by Poe to be the psychological key to its plot. Even a casual comparison of these stories will reveal not merely the similar theme of obsession but also the dominant concepts which provide the motivation in all three: the power of the psychical over the physical and the power of frustrate love to create an erotic symbolism and mythology in compensation for sensual disappointment. Although Poe grinds them differently in each story, they are the same grist to his mill.

In the interpretation of "Ligeia" particularly, an understanding of the nonrational makes necessary an almost complete reversal of certain critical opinions and explanations which assume that the story is a tale of the supernatural.... Actually, the story seems both aesthetically and psychologically more intelligible as a tale, not of supernatural, but rather of entirely natural, though highly phrenetic, psychological phenomena.

Monomania

Let us examine the personality of the hero of "Ligeia," the narrator whose psycho-emotional experience weaves the plot. He is presented in the first paragraph as a man with an erotic obsession of long standing; his wife is presumably dead, but his idolatrous devotion to her has kept her physical beauty and her personality painfully alive in his every thought. That this devotion approaches monomania becomes more clear with every statement he makes about her. She is the acme of womanly beauty and spiritual perfection. From the time of his first acquaintance with her he has been oblivious of all but her beauty and her power over him: "I cannot, for my soul, remember how, when, or even precisely where, I first became acquainted with the Lady Ligeia." Furthermore, there is his interesting admission that "I have *never known* the paternal name of her who was my friend and my betrothed, and who became the partner of my studies, and finally the wife of my bosom." In view of the fact that she was of an exceedingly ancient family and had brought him wealth "very far more, than ordinarily falls to the lot of mortals," these admissions are more than strange. Though the hero half recognizes the incongruity of his unbelievable ignorance, he dismisses it as evidence of a lover's devotion—a "wildly romantic offering on the shrine of the most passionate devotion."

Beginning with the second paragraph, we see more clearly the degree of his obsession. Although he makes much of the power of Ligeia's intellect, his imaginative preoccupation with her physical beauty is highly sensuous, even voluptuous, in its intensity. He seems to be a psychopath who has failed to find the last, final meaning of life in the coils of Ligeia's raven hair, her ivory skin, her "jetty lashes of great length," and, above all, in her eyes, "those shining, those divine orbs!" . . .

Ligeia Holds the Key to Wisdom

In this passage it is not difficult to perceive the oblique confession of inadequacy and to trace the psychological process of symbolism, which compensates for the failure of sense by apotheosis [attaining divinity] of the object of desire. Although sensuous delight leads the hero to "the very verge" of a "wisdom too divinely precious not to be forbidden," final knowledge of the secret of Ligeia's eyes is blocked by an obstacle deep within the hero's own psyche. . . .

A Psychopathic Search for Godhood

From this psychic formula derives, then, the megalomania that he can by power of will become god-like, blending his spirit with the universal spirit of deity symbolized in the divine Ligeia, who possesses in apotheosis all the attributes of his own wish, extended in a symbolic ideal beyond the touch of mortality and raised to the absoluteness of deity—intensity in thought, passion, and sensibility; perfection in wisdom, beauty, and power of mind. . . .

But the hero's approach to power is thwarted by Ligeia's death. Just at the point when triumph seems imminent, when he feels "that delicious vista by slow degrees expanding before me, down whose long, gorgeous, and all untrodden path, I might at length pass onward to the goal of a wisdom too divinely precious not to be forbidden"—just then Ligeia dies, because of the weakness of her own mortal will and in spite of the fervor with which the hero himself "struggled desperately in spirit with the grim Azrael."

At this point it may be noted that the obsession with the *idée fixe* . . . begins with the hero himself and does not express Ligeia's belief. It is his will to conquer death that motivates the rest of the story, not hers. . . .

The Madman as Narrator

In following all that the hero says, the reader must keep constantly in mind that, if the hero is suffering from obsession, his narrative cannot be accepted merely at its face value as authentic of all the facts; and he must remember that incidents and circumstances have a primary significance in terms of the hero's mania which is often at variance with the significance which the hero believes and means to convey. This is to say that Poe's psychological effect in "Ligeia" is similar to that of later delvers in psychological complexity, like Henry James, whose stories told by a narrator move on two planes. There is the story which the narrator means to tell, and there is the story which he tells without meaning to, as he unconsciously reveals himself.

Hence, the important elements in the hero's description of Ligeia are of primary significance as they reveal his feeling of psychic inadequacy, his voluptuous imagination, and his megalomania and fierce obsession with the idea that by power of will man may thwart death through spiritual love. Likewise, the narrative of the circumstances of Ligeia's death is of significance, not merely as it reveals her love of life and her struggle to live, but as it reveals the psychological crisis in which the hero's psychic shock and frustration bring on final and complete mania, the diagnostic fallacy of which is that his will is omnipotent and can bring Ligeia back to life. . . .

It is of particular importance that, with the beginning of the second half of the story, the reader keep in mind these two planes of meaning, for the primary significance of what the hero tells in this part is never in any circumstance the plain truth. It is rather an entirely, and obviously, fantastic representation of the facts, which justifies his obsessed psyche and proves that he has been right and Ligeia (and perhaps the gentle reader) wrong in the assumption that mortality is the common human fate—the old story of the madman who knows that he is right and the rest of the world wrong. . . .

False and Misleading

Up to the second half of the story, the hero has unintentionally mixed a generous amount of obliquely truthful interpretation with the facts of his story; but from this point to the end he narrates events with a pseudo-objectivity that wholly, though not necessarily intentionally, falsifies their significance. He tells what he saw and heard and felt, but these things must be understood as the hallucinations of his mania, as wish-projections which arise from his obsession with the idea of resurrecting Ligeia in the body of Rowena. He tells the effects but ignores or misrepresents the causes: he wants his audience to believe that the power of Ligeia's will effected her resurrection in the body of Rowena but does not want his audience to recognize (what he himself would not) that he was the actual agent of Rowena's death and his perceptions mere hallucinations produced by obsessional desire.

In brief, it must be recognized that the hero has murdered Rowena in his maniacal attempt to restore Ligeia to life. Although his narrative of the "sudden illness" which seized Rowena "about the second month of the marriage" avoids anything which suggests a physical attempt at murder, there are unintentional confessions of deliberate psychological cruelty in the macabre furnishings of the apartment and in the weird sounds and movements designed to produce ghostly effects. . . .

As an artist Poe depicted the functioning of both rational and nonrational processes in a character obsessed by a psychopathic desire. . . .

The hero of the story either is or is not to be completely trusted as a rational narrator whose account can be accepted with the meaning which he wishes it to have, and Poe either does or does not give the reader to understand which point of view he must take. To me, at least, Poe makes obvious the fact of the hero's original obsession in the first half of the story and his megalomania in the second half. The concluding paragraph remains aesthetically as utterly incomprehensible to me . . . if the story is merely a story of the supernatural designed to produce an impression.

Contemporary Instances of Death and Abnormal Psychology

The Obsession of the Stalker

Kathleen Megan

Kathleen Megan is a staff writer for the The Hartford Courant, *a Connecticut newspaper.*

After a Wesleyan University coed was killed, Megan examined the physical and psychological consequences of stalking. In the following article, she explains that stalking frequently is involved in cases of assault, rape, domestic violence, and murder. There is also the unrelenting fear and psychological damage to the victims of stalking, even when police and legal intervention is requested. One victim reports that "the fear never leaves." More than 3 million people aged eighteen and over are stalked in the United States every year. Three times more women are stalked than men. Stalking often consists of following a victim or confronting him or her constantly. This may include waiting for the victim in places where it is inappropriate for the stalker to be, making repeated and unwanted phone calls, or bombarding the victim with letters and gifts. Now stalking has also moved to the Internet, where the stalker can post information or spread rumors about the victim.

It doesn't matter how many locks you have on the door, how much counseling you get or even whether the criminal justice system works.

If you have been a stalking victim, "the fear never leaves," said Sherri, who changed her name because of the experience and doesn't want it published. "It's like being a prisoner of war or having your own personal terrorist. You can go somewhere where you think you are safe, but you live with the psychological damage forever."

Victims of Obsession

Every year, about 3.4 million people 18 and older are stalked in the U.S., according to the U.S. Bureau of Justice Statistics, with women three times more likely to be victimized than men. Nearly three in four stalking victims know their offender in some way.

Although it frequently goes unreported and even unrecognized, stalking is often an element in physical assault, rape and domestic violence cases, and also in murder cases such as the [May 2009] slaying of Johanna Justin-Jinich, a Wesleyan University student.

Sherri's stalker was her former husband. Although he spent time in prison for stalking and harassing her and many years have passed since he last stalked her, she still fears that what happened to Justin-Jinich could happen to her.

Justin-Jinich was gunned down at the off-campus bookstore in Middletown [Connecticut] where she worked. The suspect, Stephen P. Morgan, who has been arrested and charged with murder, took the same course as Justin-Jinich at New York University during the summer of 2007.

While at NYU, Justin-Jinich filed a harassment complaint after she said she received repeated phone calls and insulting e-mails from Morgan. According to the police report, one of those e-mails said, "You're going to have a lot more problems down the road if you can't take any [expletive] criticism, Johanna."

Both Justin-Jinich and Morgan were interviewed by police, but Morgan apparently left town and Justin-Jinich decided not to press charges.

The public doesn't know yet whether Justin-Jinich lived in fear of Morgan or if she had any idea he was tracking her down, but Sherri said she speaks out on stalking because people need to hear the message that "these guys are dangerous . . . I feel fortunate to be alive."

Under Connecticut laws passed in the early 1990s, a person is guilty of stalking if he or she "repeatedly follows or lies in wait," causing a person to reasonably fear for his physical safety.

According to a federal survey, stalking behaviors include unwanted phone calls, letters, e-mails, or gifts; spying on a victim; showing up at places without a legitimate reason; waiting at places for the victim; posting information or spreading rumors about a victim on the Internet, in a public place or by word of mouth.

Eighty-seven percent of stalkers are men. About 40 percent of men and women victims report stalking to the police. Thirty-seven percent of victims said the stalker was motivated by retaliation, anger or spite; 33 percent said it was a desire to control the victim.

Stalking Often Results in Violence

And, according to the Stalking Resource Center of the National Center for Victims of Crime, stalking is often linked to violence: Eighty-one percent of women stalked by a current or former partner are also physically assaulted by that partner; 31 percent are also sexually assaulted by that partner.

In some cases, stalking has also been linked to mass killings. The suspect in the Justin-Jinich case had written in a journal of his plans to kill Justin-Jinich and then go on a "killing spree" at Wesleyan. In the Virginia Tech case, Seung-Hui Cho was accused of stalking two women before killing 32 people [in 2007].

At the University of Connecticut, Kathy Fischer, assistant director of the Women's Center, said that several times a year students come in who are concerned about being stalked. Often, Fischer said, it's electronic stalking—instant messaging, texting and Facebook.

Robert L. Trestman, a professor of medicine and psychiatry at the University of Connecticut School of Medicine, said that there are many kinds of stalkers—from those who stalk celebrities to rejected ex-lovers and stalkers who believe that someone did them wrong, such as an ex-boss, a police officer or a judge.

In many cases, Trestman said, the stalking goes back "to the old issue: if I can't have her, nobody can. . . . Jealousy runs deep in a lot of people. Control can be a big, big piece of this and a sense that people might feel empowered by being this way to others."

Often, people don't identify what is happening to them as stalking, according to Michelle Garcia of the Stalking Resource Center in Washington.

This is because the behavior itself might not be illegal, Garcia said. She said that victims will say, "Yeah, they were calling me dozens of times a day, sending me unwanted gifts, but I didn't realize it was a crime."

Stalking, Garcia said, has become "normalized" with movies and songs that romanticize it.

"Most of the messages out there are: This is rather fun, romantic, it's not a big deal," said Garcia, instead of: "This is something dangerous, something that could be lethal."

Patricide Without Remorse

Manuel Roig-Franzia

Manuel Roig-Franzia is a Mexico City–based Washington Post *staff writer whose beat is Latin America.*

In the following selection, Roig-Franzia recounts the details of a patricide, or killing of one's own father. Bill Bond, who grew up with his twin, Richard, still remembers being regarded as the bad twin, harassed daily by a father who called him no good and worthless. He was in constant trouble as a teenager. After his parents divorced, his mother continued to compare him unfavorably with his twin brother and, when he was seventeen, demanded that he leave her house in Ohio and go to live with his father in Georgia. His father came to pick him up but told him before they began the trip that he did not want Bill to live with him. Bill responded by smashing his father's skull with a hammer. This occurred thirty years ago, and Bill's only sentence was to be treated as a juvenile in a Baltimore psychiatric hospital for a time. Like Poe's murderers, Bill was compelled to confess his crime in detail in an autobiography, which is being kept under seal in court because of its relevance to a custody case.

The killer at middle age lives in a stately Georgian colonial in a swanky Baltimore neighborhood.

He pads in his socks across Persian carpet. He passes the leather sofas arranged by his interior designer in a living room where classical music is almost always playing.

A Flash of Violence

The tranquil ambiance offers no hint of the defining moment of Bill Bond's life: a sudden flash of teen violence nearly three decades ago that he once tried to profit from and has never denied.

Rather than occupying a prison cell, Bond has spent most of his adult life among Baltimore's elite, playing tennis at the finest clubs, dining at French bistros, schmoozing at gourmet groceries, walking his Briard showdog, Magic.

But anxiety has entered Bond's carefully constructed world.

He's lost his heiress wife, whose wealth, along with his own inheritances, helped him indulge in the good life without a paying job before their separation. He's lost a long legal battle aimed at preserving control of the untold story of his dark history—a complicated copyright dispute that he pursued, unsuccessfully, all the way to the U.S. Supreme Court [in 2009].

Now he's about to lose his finest wine.

"I'm not going to watch this," he says, turning his back and pacing.

Even more off-limits is the box at the opposite end of the basement. Inside is a 600-page manuscript that has never been published. Once, it amounted to an attempt to explain himself and make him as rich as the people around him.

But Bond can't truly be understood without going back to the beginning, to a small town in Ohio, where he was a bright, athletic, angry teenager. A twin everyone called Billy.

The "Bad" Twin

Billy and his twin, Richard, lived privileged lives in Chagrin Falls, Ohio, a Cleveland suburb. Their mother, whose maiden name is Elizabeth Johnson, came from old money, locals say. Their father, Mirko Rovtar Jr., hailed from a Slovenian immigrant family who had built a business but lacked high-society bona fides.

Billy, who changed his last name to Bond as an adult, attended private school. There were Caribbean vacations and tennis lessons. In photographs from the 1970s, he and his brother wear stylish clothes, looking tanned and happy.

Bond now stands at 5-foot-8 and weighs 180 pounds, chiseled by biweekly boxing workouts, distance cycling and ping-pong lessons with a former Soviet national team coach.

Forty-five and balding, he no longer flaunts the blond locks that once made him look like tennis star Bjorn Borg. He has a sardonic wit and flirts habitually.

He is reluctant to talk about his childhood but hints at class conflicts roiling his family. His parents met, he says, at Transylvania University, a small, liberal arts college in Lexington, Ky. His mother's parents were not pleased when she became pregnant, Bond says.

The birth of twin boys did not make things easier. He describes his father as tall and "very good-looking," but distant and unloving.

"What's worse?" Bond asks. "I hit you one time in my kitchen, or every day for 10 years I tell you, 'You're no good.'"

By the late 1970s, his parents' marriage had unraveled. His father, who had operated a successful insulation business and worked in the chemical industry, had moved to Georgia. At home in Ohio, Billy clashed with his mother, accusing her of favoring his twin brother.

"I was the bad one," Bond says. She finally demanded that he live with his father, Bond recalls. He was 17 when his father came to pick him up in June 1981.

The Murder

"It was in the fall of my junior year when Ricky and I (had begun) talking, over ping-pong, of killing dad," Bond wrote in his manuscript. "We both became infatuated with the idea, and we talked about it all the time. My mother did tell us not to discuss things like that . . . but Ricky and I definitely got the impression from her that it wouldn't be such a terrible thing if dad was dead."

Bond said his manuscript is a "highly fictionalized . . . stylized" account, but Maryland courts have said the work's outline tracks the facts.

Bond's mother and his brother, Richard Johnson, an attorney, could not be reached for comment. Richard Johnson denied to the *Washington Post* in 2001 that he had plotted with his brother to kill their father.

Before they could leave for Georgia, Billy argued with his father in the garage at the home of his grandfather, Mirko Rovtar Sr., in nearby Bainbridge, Ohio. Bond says his father told him: "I don't want you to come live with me. I never wanted to have you."

Billy responded by smashing his father's skull with a hammer.

"I see the garage bathed in shadowy light, my father lying in a pool of his own blood, and, for the first time, I can see myself quite clearly. I am filled with vanity," Bond wrote.

A Maryland appeals court gave more details, paraphrasing Bond's manuscript—which has been kept under seal in a Baltimore courthouse after being used in a custody case related to Bond's stepchildren. The court said he wrote of "how his dying father attempted to raise himself off the floor of the garage before Bond delivered the final blows to his neck and head. (The manuscript) describes Bond wiping away his fingerprints, scrubbing the garage floor, cleaning blood, flesh and bone from his clothes."

The body was found in his father's car, parked near a convenience store on the edge of town, says Bainbridge Police Chief Jim Jimison, who investigated the crime. Blood dripped from the trunk. Police discovered a note that suggested Rovtar was killed in a dispute over illegal drugs, but police weren't buying it, Jimison says.

While police looked for clues, Billy went to a concert with a friend. Police questioned him the next day. He failed a polygraph, Jimison says, but "there was no repentance."

"That's what really bothers you," Jimison says. "Only person in my career that when the evidence is put forward and the jig is up, who wasn't able to show some remorse. You talk about calculating and selfish."

The motive was uncertain. Quotes from Bond's manuscript indicate that he killed his father to gain an inheritance. Indeed, Bond acknowledges that he later inherited money from his father's estate.

Bond says he eventually was "found delinquent" as part of a deal with prosecutors to keep the case in the juvenile court system. He had killed his father eight months before his 18th birthday. Instead of going to prison, he was ordered to receive treatment at Sheppard Pratt, a Baltimore psychiatric hospital.

"He got off far too easy," Jimison says. "In my opinion, he should still be in prison. It seems like he went from riches to riches."

My Family Was Sick

Bond steers his BMW onto the grounds of Sheppard Pratt.

"That's where I lived," he says, nodding up at a sterile-looking building. "Hall C7."

Many of the teens at Sheppard Pratt were drug abusers or fighting through emotional troubles, he says. He doesn't recall other teen killers: "I was very unusual."

"In group therapy," he says, "I wasn't allowed to discuss why I was there. I'd get all the crazy kids upset."

He remembers only one visit from his mother, and two from his father's parents, who would give him money from time to time. In the years since, he has had an on-again-off-again relationship with his mother. He is estranged from his twin brother.

"The whole family was sick," Bond says. "I'm glad I got out of it. For all intents and purposes, I've lost them as a family, and I'm glad."

At Sheppard Pratt, Billy formed a bond with one of his psychiatrists, Kay Koller, who would drive him to tennis clubs and helped prepare him for life outside the facility. Released after 10 months, tennis gave the young Bond exposure to people of means in Baltimore—he taught lessons at clubs and resurfaced courts.

"I made myself likable," he says.

A Book of Confession

In the winters, Bond traveled, spending months in Brazil and Central America. He also visited Jamaica, where he fell in with a well-to-do crowd. Friends set him up with a house in Port Antonio, Jamaica, the very house, he says, where Robin Moore wrote "The French Connection." It was there, in 1987, he says, that he set out to write his own best-seller.

Over seven years, Bond's manuscript "went from fiction to non-fiction" to fiction again, he explains. "By the time it went through this, it was Truman Capote fiction-non-fiction. . . ."

Bond attracted the attention of a literary manager, Ken Atchity. They met in the early 1990s in New York, Atchity recalls, and Bond was "very charismatic and persuasive. . . . You would never have thought we were sitting there talking about murder. He was very crisp and matter-of-fact about it."

Atchity's firm later produced promotional materials for a book called "Self-Portrait of a Patricide: How I Got Away with Murder." But Atchity couldn't get a publisher interested, and he soured on Bond.

The manuscript "was self-justifying, flat, emotionless, almost like he was in the audience watching somebody onstage," Atchity reflects.

"Did he change" after the murder? Atchity asks. "In this case, the answer is no. . . . He wasn't feeling the dark night of the soul that one would expect."

A Marriage Leads to Court Battles

In 1995, Bond began dating a mom of three named Alyson Slavin, who owned an antiques store. He shared his manuscript with her, he says, and moved that same year into her 8,000-square-foot home in Guilford.

Alyson is the daughter of Kenneth Blum, co-founder of Baltimore-based United Healthcare. In March 1996, Bond sent Blum an extraordinary letter asking for a "dowry" before he would marry Alyson. Along with the dowry, Bond asked for a studio apartment, a salary to compensate him for helping Alyson with her family problems and the promise of a severance package if the marriage broke up.

"You can pay me now or pay me later," he said.

The letter, particularly the request for a dowry, incensed Alyson's father.

"That says it all," says Blum, now 82 and retired in Boca Raton, Fla. "At best, I would say he's very strange."

Blum had been giving Alyson $200,000 a year for living expenses and paid for her children's private education, according to court records. He eventually hired a private investigator to look into Bond's past.

Despite her father's fury, Alyson married Bond on May 8, 2001. About that time, the investigator acquired a copy of the manuscript from the widow of Bond's former attorney. That discovery, along with the investigator's acquisition of Bond's Ohio juvenile record, set off a chain of events that has played out in Maryland courts ever since.

The grudge match between Bond and Blum has cost Bond $600,000 in legal fees and threatened his financial stability. Along the way, Bond has accused some of Maryland's most prominent lawyers and judges of all sorts of shenanigans.

After Bond's manuscript was found, he was arrested for allegedly lying on a gun-purchase application about whether he had been in a mental institution. (The charges were dismissed.) Back then, Bond says, he seldom left the house without a weapon, a habit from his days in Jamaica.

About the time of the gun issue, attorneys for Alyson's first husband, William Slavin, tried to introduce the manuscript as evidence in a custody dispute. Slavin said he was concerned about his 14- and 12-year-old daughters living with Bond.

Bond tried to block the manuscript from being used by filing a copyright infringement lawsuit, which he lost. (In the years since, Bond has continued asking for attorneys' fees and damages of more than $140 million, and he also has failed to prevail on claims that Blum, U.S. District Judge Marvin Garbis, attorney Gerald Martin and others rigged cases against him.)

Despite the introduction of the manuscript in the child-custody case, Alyson Slavin Bond retained physical custody of her minor children. But Bond says the family was riven by resentments and discipline problems, and the next year, he and his wife sent the children to live with their father.

Alyson, now 53, did not return calls. [At this writing the couple was getting divorced.] Her father says Bond "destroyed her life."

As the court fight went on, the couple wasn't as flush with cash as before. Alyson's father cut off financial support. The couple remained in Guilford, but they downsized to a 2,500-square-foot house.

Few neighbors knew about Bond's history, and those who did weren't particularly bothered by it.

"I don't think anybody who knows him focuses on that," Howard Friedel, head of the Guilford homeowners association, says of Bond's criminal past. "He's been a positive individual in the community."

Without Remorse

On his office counter, there is list of goals for 2009, among them, finding "Mrs. Right!!!!!"

Mrs. Right would resemble the wife of agent Ari Gold on HBO's "Entourage"—"minus the temper," Bond says. Or, maybe, the Playboy model Shauna Sand "sans the insecurity."

"When I put all these qualifications into Match.com, I had zero matches for the entire United States, which made me laugh very hard, then cry," Bond says. He didn't put "father killer" into his Match.com profile. But he knows that label is with him forever.

"I wish I wouldn't have done it," he says one day after much prodding. "Not because I miss my father so much, but because of what I did to myself."

Journey of a Schizophrenic

Elyn R. Saks

Elyn R. Saks is associate dean and the Orrin B. Evans Professor of Law, Psychology, and Psychiatry and the Behavioral Sciences at the University of Southern California School of Law and an adjunct professor of psychiatry at the University of California–San Diego School of Medicine.

Saks, in documenting her "journey through madness," relates an episode when she decided to stop taking her medications during her stay in a mental hospital. She had by this time been in and out of numerous psychiatric facilities and received varying diagnoses and medications. She details her symptoms over the years: rocking and humming during therapy sessions, hallucinating, having delusions, threatening harm to others, and babbling incoherently. After the drugs lessened the psychosis, deep depression set in, and she was transferred to yet another hospital. A diagnosis of schizophrenia, a withdrawal from antipsychotic drugs, and her family's insistence that she could cure herself if she really tried led her to realize that the journey before her would be a long one.

The first patient I met once back at YPI [Yale Psychiatric Institute] was Eric. An Ivy League graduate slightly older than I, Eric, too, had spent time on MU10 [Mental Unit 10]. "I was there a little over a year ago, but they let me go," he told me. "I wish they'd made me stay, and then maybe moved me here, like they did with you. I fooled them into thinking I was OK. And I went home. And then I killed my father."

Surely I'd misheard him. "I'm sorry, you did what?"

He nodded. "I strangled him."

I was dumbstruck. And horrified. To actually strangle your father? A laying on of hands that actually kills someone? That was, very different from having thoughts that could kill. Besides, entities worked *through* me; Eric, it seemed, was his own agent.

In the Mental Institution

My parents came back from Miami for the first meeting of my YPI care team—doctors, psychologists, social workers, and nurses. When asked about my relationship with my brother Warren, I stopped rocking and humming long enough to correct the inquiring doctor's grammar. "No, it's 'between you and me,' not 'between you and I.'" I can only imagine now (but was completely oblivious at the time) that it must have been sheer torture for my mother and father to witness the worsening disintegration of their daughter.

I was placed in YPI's Intensive Care Program—ICP. My days would be spent in a small room with a staff member and one or two other ICP patients. I would take my meals apart from everyone else (no socializing for me in the cafeteria) and sleep in a locked seclusion room at night. And I was not allowed to wear shoes. That way, if I escaped the building, staff could be certain I wouldn't get too far. The New England autumn was deepening outside, and it was getting colder every day. . . .

My medication was increased, putting me over the maximum recommended dose for Trilafon. No Valium, though—it seemed that staff wanted me on meds that actually helped my psychosis.

Symptoms of the Psychotic

Nevertheless, the hallucinations never stopped. Walls were collapsing, ashtrays were dancing; at one point I went into a linen closet and invited the other ICP patients to join me in there for a "housewarming" party, as I laughed and gibbered the afternoon away. Totally lost in my delusions, I warned of the great horrors and devastation that I could inflict upon everyone (most notably the ICP staff) with the power of my mind. . . .

Every day was the same, and would be for a long time. The years yawned out ahead of me; my hair would turn gray here, I knew it, while every dream I'd ever had would be absorbed into the ugly yellowed walls.

And then something threw a switch in my head, and I got it. I *got* it. The only barrier between me and the door out was me. I simply had to *stop* it. Stop voicing the hallucinations and delusions, even when they were there. Stop babbling incoherently, even if those were the only words that came to my lips; no, no, it was better to be quiet. Stop resisting; just behave. *Being in a psychiatric hospital is nonsense,* I thought. *I'm a law student, not a mental patient. I want my life back, damn it! And if I have to bite my tongue until it bleeds, I am going to get it back.*

What was happening, of course, was that after weeks of steady medication, the psychosis was beginning to lift. Maybe I couldn't keep the thoughts from coming into my head, but I could organize them, and keep them from getting out. *OK, here I go.*

It took staff a week or so to notice—much too long, it seemed to me—and when they finally did, it took another week before I was off the Intensive Care Program and allowed more privileges. I could sleep with socks. I could use the bathroom in peace. I could shower without company. . . .

As sudden (and effective) as I thought my change in attitude had been, what happened to me next was just as sudden, only in the reverse direction. In fact, it's a case study—partly—in the ups and downs of heavy drug loads and the complicated biochemistry that results: Soaked in antipsychotic medication, with the psychosis actually clearing, I became profoundly depressed, and felt the brief flash of energy and

With the help of steady medication, a mental patient's psychosis can begin to lift. AP Images.

focus leak right out of me. Suddenly, I couldn't follow the simplest sitcom on the unit TV, or decipher the lines in a book I'd been reading just days before. I was given an IQ test and scored "dull normal" in the verbal portion and "borderline mentally retarded" in the quantitative section. It's not that I wasn't trying—I just couldn't function. I had no way of knowing that depression following a psychotic period is not unusual; I only knew I was sliding backward. I called my parents and pleaded with them to get me out. "It's all going wrong again!" I cried. . . .

Yet Another Hospital

The Institute of Pennsylvania Hospital—IPH—was a much more physically attractive place than YPI, in spite of being the oldest mental hospital in the country. Located smack in the middle of a neighborhood in serious decline, the building literally shone, with high, vaulted ceilings and marble floors that were polished daily. I was taken to my private room, with its own private bath. If there was a food chain of treatment centers, it appeared as though I'd moved up. Although I was still trying to get out from under the depression, I was nowhere near as psychotic as I had been (thanks to the hefty dose of Trilafon). I was convinced that I'd only be at IPH a couple of weeks. In the end, it would be three months. . . .

Going off Meds

In spite of the side effects, I had to admit that the Trilafon was helping. Nevertheless, I was, as always, anxious to get off meds. Karen [my therapist] was rabidly anti-medication as well, and my parents were, too, so [my psychoanalyst Dr.] Miller agreed that we could give it a try, but very slowly.

As cautious as he was in reducing my intake, I felt the effects almost immediately. My blank, masklike face relaxed into its familiar appearance, and I stopped doing the invalid shuffle down the hall. I felt less fuzzy, more aware of what was going on around me. "You seem angrier to me, though," said Miller. I'd walked out of a couple of sessions before we'd officially ended, which concerned him.

"I can handle it," I said, impatient. "Let's keep going."

In two months, I was med-free, except for something to help me sleep. At three months, I was one of the old-timers on the ward. In fact, the staff sometimes consulted me in ward meetings about newer patients—which one was doing OK, which one needed watching, and who might deserve more privileges. I wasn't comfortable with this role: Was I a colleague to them? Was I still a patient and, if so, why did they trust me? And which of them could I trust? I'd have preferred being left out of it entirely. But I knew that every move I made was still being closely watched; if I was nonresponsive when asked my opinion, I knew I'd pay some kind of price. Once, walking down the hall, I jumped up to touch the ceiling, just to see if I could—and then caught myself, panicky about what would happen if I'd been seen. I'd be written up.

My fear of being scrutinized wasn't paranoia. Others really were watching me, and the risk was real. . . .

As I walked down the hall on my last day, suitcase in hand, one of the custodians who came to the ward daily, a good-looking, wiry man, saw me. Although we'd never had a single exchange during my entire stay, this time he smiled warmly and nodded at the suitcase. "Good for you, getting out."

My own smile stretched as wide as his did. "Thank you," I said and walked out into the late spring sunshine.

In the taxi on the way to the Philadelphia airport, however, the sense of having made my escape and leaving the hospital behind was more than I could handle. I was alone, and unguarded, and as the emotions piled on top of one another, I was quickly overwhelmed by them. As though they'd slipped by a guard at the gate, the delusions marched in—paranoid thoughts and a strong message from someone, something, insistent upon being heard. I was the center of a massive and intricate plot involving the creatures in the sky. It would somehow involve the plane I was about to take. But the idea of returning to the hospital never crossed my mind. Gritting my teeth, and trying with all my might to focus on what I knew to be real, I grimly boarded the plane for Miami. *Hold it together. Hold it together.* It was, as usual, an uneventful flight.

The Constant Struggle

It was May and I was home, just as a lot of other young people were at the end of a year away at school. September to May— one full academic year since I'd walked across the Yale campus sporting a telephone-wire belt and babbling about my complicity in the impending end of the world. And now here I was back home again, completely off antipsychotic meds and somewhat functional, although just barely on some days. Good days, bad days. More bad days. I went to the beach with my brother and sister-in-law, and the light and heat almost made me cower. In minutes, I was convinced that everyone there had come to the beach to ambush me—they thought I was evil, that I had killed many people. I was certain that if I moved suddenly, they'd leap up and kill me. I sat stiff as a board on my towel down near the water, silently begging not to be noticed. I wished I had brought a gun with me to protect myself in case I was attacked.

Years of this illness had taken a toll. The constant effort to keep reality on one side and delusions on the other was exhausting, and I often felt beaten down, knowing that the schizophrenia diagnosis had ended any hope I'd had of a miracle cure or a miracle fix.

The Insanity Defense

Lara Bricker

Lara Bricker is an award-winning investigative reporter and writer whose work appears in many publications, including The Boston Globe, The Portsmouth Herald, *and* The Exeter News-Letter.

In the following selection, Bricker reports that no matter how unstable criminals may appear in court, juries are very unlikely to accept an insanity plea. Murderers have confessed in court that God or other voices ordered them to commit crimes and have used their own abusive childhoods as reasons for insanity pleas. The insanity defense is used in less than 1 percent of cases nationally and is overwhelmingly unsuccessful. If both the prosecution and defense determine that the criminal is insane, the case usually does not go to trial. The law does not clarify what constitutes insanity so it is the responsibility of the jury to listen to experts brought forward by both the defense and the prosecution and to determine for themselves the validity of the insanity plea. One difficulty, according to an attorney, is that juries generally believe that those on trial fake their insanity.

The rarely used insanity defense brought into play in the case of Sheila LaBarre has not worked for a handful of other murder defendants in the state [of New Hampshire].

The Insanity Plea

One heard God tell him to kill his wife and son. Another, with an abusive childhood, snapped when he strangled his wife and suffocated his three children. Both did as LaBarre, 49, has opted to do in their murder cases, when they waived the guilt

Lara Bricker, "Sheila LaBarre: Poster Child for Insanity Defense?" Seacoastonline.com, February 17, 2008. Reproduced by permission.

phase of the case and moved straight to a trial on their sanity. Both failed to convince a jury they were insane at the time of the slayings and are now serving life sentences.

"It's been tried and it is an uphill battle. It's not an easy thing," said Manchester lawyer Michael Ramsdell, a former head of the homicide unit at the state Attorney General's Office and a former federal prosecutor, who added that LaBarre's decision is a rare move. "It's not unprecedented, but it is unusual."

In LaBarre's favor is the fact that both of her two lead attorneys have handled previous insanity cases and one of those attorneys, Jeffrey Denner, has successfully tried a case in which his client was found not guilty by reason of insanity.

The insanity defense is used in less than 1 percent of cases nationally and rarely successful, according to Gregory Hurley, a spokesperson for the National Center for State Courts, which collects data from cases nationally.

But LaBarre's attorneys are vocal in their belief that their client was completely and utterly insane when she killed Kenneth Countie, 24, of Massachusetts, and Michael Deloge, 37, of Somersworth.

As part of a not guilty by reason of insanity plea, LaBarre, 49, admitted that prosecutors had enough evidence to prove that she killed Countie and then burned his body and that she also killed Deloge.

Delusions and Murder

Prosecutors have not offered a theory for the manner in which Deloge was killed, but have witnesses who report seeing LaBarre beat Deloge and DNA evidence that blood inside the house was likely from Deloge. In both cases, LaBarre accused the men, her lovers at the time, of being pedophiles and has made statements that she was an angel brought to kill pedophiles.

While her attorneys won't reveal details on the results of a psychological evaluation of LaBarre, Denner said recently she could become the poster child for insanity defense cases.

"There is a clearly defined standard that must be proven in insanity cases in New Hampshire, and we believe that our client and the evidence in this case will allow us to meet that standard," said attorney Brad Bailey.

How the Insanity Law Works

New Hampshire's law with regard to insanity in criminal cases uses a two-pronged test to determine whether a defendant is not guilty by reason of insanity, explained Exeter lawyer Rich Taylor, who with his partner, Alex Yiokarinis, was brought onto LaBarre's defense team.

The burden is on the defense to present a case to prove insanity. That is why the defense goes first in an insanity trial, the opposite of a usual trial.

The defense must first show that LaBarre suffered from a mental disease or defect. Then, it must show the murders were a product of that mental disease or defect. Neither "mental disease" or "defect" has been defined by the Legislature or the courts, Taylor said, which means it is up to the jury to decide whether the evidence presented about LaBarre qualifies.

"It's going to be a determination made by the jury, and it's not going to be a determination made by an expert witness," Taylor said. "The expert witness cannot offer an opinion at trial on the ultimate question of whether or not the defendant could have formed the mental state during the moment of the crime."

New Hampshire's law empowers the jury more than in other states where there are elaborate definitions of what qualifies as insanity, said Albert "Buzz" Scherr, a lawyer and professor at Franklin Pierce Law Center and former defense attorney.

If a jury finds LaBarre had a mental disease or defect, it does not have to find her not guilty, Ramsdell said, adding there could be a motive for the murder other than the mental illness. A jury would also consider if LaBarre has been previously diagnosed with a mental illness or whether she was recently diagnosed as part of the evaluation of this case.

LaBarre's attorneys originally planned to proceed with a bifurcated trial, which means she would have first gone to trial on her guilt or innocence, and then, if found guilty, had a second phase on her sanity. Going forward with just the insanity portion of the trial is a strategic move, Scherr said, as it will lessen the amount of time the jury hears the evidence in the trial, which in LaBarre's case is gruesome.

Also, the type of evidence presented in the insanity trial will not be as detailed in some areas that would have been more in-depth at a trial on guilt or innocence, such as a medical examiner's report, he explained.

"The prosecution will not be allowed to go into ... exquisite detail," Scherr said. "It's a mechanism for controlling the extent of emotionally disturbing evidence that the jury will hear."

A jury would also be less likely to find someone insane if it had already found him/her guilty.

"If you've already found somebody guilty, are you going to be more or less likely to find them insane? It's just natural human instinct," Scherr said.

Ramsdell agreed, pointing out that if a jury already rejects the defense arguments related to the first-degree murder charges, it is already rejecting some of the same defense positions that might enter the sanity portion of a case.

"It's undoubtedly a strategic decision," he said of bypassing the guilt phase of the case.

Juries Suspect Insanity Pleas

The number of trials that go forward with an insanity defense is misleading with regard to the potential number of insanity cases, Ramsdell said.

In some cases when the issue of sanity is raised, the prosecution has its own expert evaluate the defendant. If the state's expert concludes there was a valid basis for the insanity defense, the two sides can agree to a not guilty by reason of insanity plea without a trial, with that person being committed to a psychiatric facility.

"The state doesn't have any interest in prosecuting anybody they legitimately believe was suffering from a mental illness," Ramsdell said.

In LaBarre's case, the prosecution has had its own psychological evaluation of LaBarre done, but that report is not being made public.

Several insanity cases have gone forward in the state in recent years, including that of James Colbert, who in 1991 strangled his wife and suffocated his three young daughters in their Concord apartment.

Ramsdell prosecuted the case and Scherr represented Colbert, who was convicted and is serving a life sentence.

Colbert had a history of being seriously sexually abused through his teenage years, Scherr said. A trucker, Colbert allegedly snapped when his truck was repossessed, his wife left him and he lost his job.

The case of Robert Blair, which Ramsdell also prosecuted, was another unsuccessful insanity case. Blair bludgeoned his wife and handicapped son to death with a hammer in a Concord hotel room in March 1996.

According to Blair's appeal with the state Supreme Court, while asleep in the hotel room, he said he went into a trance in which God told him he would be "cast into the lake of fire" if he didn't kill his family. He then heard the voice of an angel command him.

Blair testified in his own defense and told the court, "In my opinion, I'm sane. I acted under the command of God," according to court documents.

Another challenge with mounting an insanity defense is the public perception that a person is faking a mental illness or trying to "get off" on a technicality, Scherr said.

Even if LaBarre is found not guilty by reason of insanity, she would most likely be committed to the secure psychiatric unit of the New Hampshire State Prison and would not be set free.

"I think juries come into a case when there's an insanity defense predisposed to not believing and it's hard to overcome that," Scherr said. "And it's even harder to overcome it when the burden's on the defense."

Bailey said he did not want to get into specifics about the public perceptions about mental illnesses. He did say the defense would raise questions with prospective jurors that would expose any feelings or prejudices about the mentally ill during their jury selection.

Some have called LaBarre a very intelligent woman capable of faking, which Scherr said is a misconception about the insane.

"The history of intelligent insane people is long, deep and rich. I don't know how many paranoid schizophrenics I've represented who are remarkably bright. People who are mentally ill are not stupid people. One's level of intelligence does not tell you anything about whether they're mentally ill."

For Further Discussion

1. Examine the psychological traumas in Edgar Allan Poe's life and how they may or may not have influenced his work. (See Meyers, Carlson, Peeples, and Morrison.)

2. In your estimation, are Poe's murderous narrators not guilty by reason of insanity or should they be punished to the full extent of the law? Explain your answer. (See Buranelli, Cleman, and Bricker.)

3. Describe Poe's characterization of women. Note that they are presented as both ideally obedient and strong and terrifying. (See Symons, Weekes, and Davidson.)

4. Discuss the physical objects on which Poe's narrators become fixated. How do you interpret them? (See May, Benfey, Davidson, and Basler.)

5. How are death and insanity related? Cite from the articles in your answer. (See May, Davidson, Weekes, and Fisher.)

6. Discuss the relevance of Poe's psychology to current cases of schizophrenia, obsession, and murder. (See Megan, Roig-Franzia, and Saks.)

For Further Reading

Jane Austen, *Northanger Abbey.* 1818.

Johann von Goethe, *Faust.* 1808–32.

Washington Irving, *"The Legend of Sleepy Hollow,"* in *The Sketch Book of Geoffrey Crayon, Gent.* 1819.

Edgar Allan Poe, *Al Araaf, Tamerlane, and Minor Poems.* 1829.

———, *Eureka: A Prose Poem.* 1848.

———, *The Narrative of Arthur Gordon Pym of Nantucket.* 1838.

———, *Poems.* 1831.

———, *The Raven and Other Poems.* 1845.

———, *Tales by Edgar A. Poe.* 1845.

———, *Tales of the Grotesque and Arabesque.* 1840.

———, *Tamerlane and Other Poems.* 1827.

Mary Shelley, *Frankenstein; or, The Modern Prometheus.* 1818.

Bibliography

Books

Jonathan S. Abramowitz, Dean McKay, and Steven Taylor, eds. *Clinical Handbook of Obsessive-Compulsive Disorder and Related Problems*. Baltimore: Johns Hopkins University Press, 2008.

Elias Aboujaoude *Compulsive Acts: A Psychiatrist's Tales of Ritual and Obsession*. Berkeley and Los Angeles: University of California Press, 2008.

Hervey Allen *Israfel: The Life and Times of Edgar Allan Poe*. 2 vols. New York: Doran, 1926.

Marie Bonaparte *Life and Works of Edgar Allan Poe: A Psycho-Analytic Interpretation*. London: Imago, 1949.

Joan Dayan *Fables of the Mind: An Inquiry into Poe's Fiction*. New York: Oxford University Press, 1987.

Jennifer L. Dunn *Courting Disaster: Intimate Stalking, Culture, and Criminal Justice*. New Brunswick, NJ: AldineTransaction, 2008.

Roger Forclaz "Psychoanalysis and Edgar Allan Poe," in *Critical Essays on Edgar Allan Poe*. Ed. Eric Carlson. Boston: G.K. Hall, 1987.

Howard Haycraft   *Murder for Pleasure.* New York and
                    London: D. Appleton-Century, 1941.

J. Gerald Kennedy   *Poe, Death, and the Life of Writing.*
                    New Haven, CT: Yale University
                    Press, 1987.

David Ketterer   *The Rationale of Deception in Poe.*
                    Baton Rouge: Louisiana State
                    University Press, 1979.

Reid Kimbrough   *The Stalking Phenomenon: Preying on
                    the Soul.* Jackson: University of North
                    Florida Press, 2001.

Bettina L. Knapp   *Edgar Allan Poe.* New York: Ungar,
                    1984.

Harry Levin   *The Power of Blackness: Hawthorne,
                    Poe, Melville.* New York: Knopf, 1958.

Allen Tate   *The Forlorn Demon: Didactic and
                    Critical Essays.* Chicago: Ayer, 1953.

Dwight Thomas   *The Poe Log: A Documentary Life of
and David K.   Edgar Allan Poe, 1809–1949.* Boston:
Jackson   G.K. Hall, 1987.

G.R. Thompson   *Poe's Fiction: Romantic Irony in the
                    Gothic Tales.* Madison: University of
                    Wisconsin Press, 1973.

Edward   *Edgar Allan Poe: The Man Behind the
Wagenknecht   Legend.* New York: Oxford University
                    Press, 1963.

Periodicals

Virginia Adams   "Psychology of Murder," *Time*, April 24, 1972.

Jacob Rama Berman   "Domestic Terror and Poe's Arabesque Interior," *English Studies in Canada*, March 2005.

Martin Bickman   "Animatopoeia: Morella as a Siren of the Self," *Poe Studies*, December 1975.

Sarah Burge   "Homeland Man Accused of Murder After Assaulted Dad Dies," *Riverside (CA) Press Enterprise*, April 27, 2009. www.pe.com.

Benedict Carey   "When the Imp in Your Brain Gets Out," *Sarasota (FL) Herald Tribune*, July 13, 2009. www.heraldtribune.com.

Ottavio Casale   "Poe's Transcendentalism," *ESQ*, vol. 50, 1968.

Richard Finholt   "The Vision at the Brink of the Abyss," *Georgia Review*, Fall 1979.

Alan Freeman   "The Killer's Message," *Globe & Mail* (Toronto), April 19, 2007.

James W. Gargano   "'The Cask of Amontillado': A Masquerade of Motive and Identity," *Studies in Short Fiction*, vol. 4, 1967.

James W. Gargano   "The Question of Poe's Narrators," *College English*, February 1963.

Diane Hoeveler — "The Hidden God and the Abjected Woman in 'The Fall of the House of Usher,'" *Studies in Short Fiction*, Summer 1992.

J.A. Leo Lemay — "The Psychology of 'The Murders in the Rue Morgue,'" *American Literature*, May 1982.

Leila S. May — "'Sympathies of a Scarcely Intelligible Nature': The Brother-Sister Bond in Poe's 'Fall of the House of Usher,'" *Short Fiction*, Summer 1993.

Joseph J. Modenhauer — "Murder as a Fine Art: Basic Connections Between Poe's Aesthetics, Psychology, and Moral Vision," *PMLA*, May 1968.

Stephen L. Mooney — "Poe's Gothic Waste Land," *Sewanee Review*, January–March 1962.

Lowery Nelson Jr. — "Night Thoughts on the Gothic Novel," *Yale Review*, vol. 3, 1962.

Dave Smith — "Edgar A. Poe and the Nightmare Ode," *Southern Humanities Review*, Winter 1995.

Richard E. Vatz — "The Devil Made Them Do It," *USA Today*, March 2007.

Shankar Vedantam — "A Social Theory of Violence Looks Beyond the Shooter," *Washington Post*, April 23, 2007.

Richard Wilbur — "The Poe Mystery Case," *New York Review of Books*, July 1967.

Index